WAR CORRESPONDENT

Also by the same author:

People at War 1914–1918
People at War 1939–1945
A Place Called Armageddon
A Yank in Bomber Command
Black Bread and Barbed Wire
Greater Love
God on Our Side

WAR CORRESPONDENT

by

MICHAEL MOYNIHAN

LEO COOPER
LONDON

First published in 1994 by
LEO COOPER
an imprint of
Pen & Sword Books Ltd,
47 Church Street, Barnsley, South Yorkshire S70 2AS

Copyright © Michael Moynihan, 1994

A CIP catalogue record for this book is available
from the British Library

ISBN 0 85052 413 X

Typset by Chippendale Type Ltd,
Otley, West Yorkshire
in Linotron 10pt Plantin

Printed by Redwood Books,
Trowbridge, Wilts

TO LISA

CONTENTS

FOREWORD

The privilege of witnessing action in all three services during the Second World War, a civilian disguised in turn in the uniforms of the air force, army and navy, came my way only because I had been officially classified as a potential liability. Called up for a medical at the outset of the war, I had never imagined that the boyhood asthma I had largely outgrown would result in a 'GRADE III (three)' in red ink on a buff certificate and the chairman of the examiners' curt "You will not be required". In the event I saw a great deal more of the war than I would otherwise have done, without once being hors de combat.

The chapters covering my eighteen months as a war correspondent, from Normandy to Japan, are based on diaries, letters and despatches (many of them, in those space-starved days, unused) and follow the pattern of seven war books I edited during the 1970s, the material for which came from the Imperial War Museum's Department of Documents.

The task of fleshing out characters from the records they left, and from what I could find out about them, presented different problems when dealing with myself. Memory can be fickle and I have relied to a large extent on what I wrote at the time. For the rest, looking back over fifty years or more, it has been possible to see my younger self with a degree of objectivity, something of an innocent abroad due to my upbringing, fortunate to have had experiences thrust upon me.

CHAPTER ONE

Kathleen Carpenter came unexpectedly to tea the Sunday war was declared. We had it on the front lawn in the shade of the hawthorn and laburnum and through their branches glimpsed the barrage balloons riding at anchor in the blue.

The black-out curtains had long been in readiness but we had just squashed more putty around the basement grilles, where gas might be expected to settle and infiltrate. For ten minutes or so every evening we had been practising wearing our gas-masks and the drawing-room was full of strangled grunts as we viewed each other, a family circle of surrealist pigs.

Miss Carpenter was absolutely for the war but was somewhat grieved that the timing had meant the abandonment of the British Association conference in Dundee, where she was to have read a paper on perch. She had brought with her an expert on animal foods, his son and his son's fiancée, who now sipped tea and nibbled cucumber sandwiches, a bit out of the chatter.

An occasional visitor to our Birkenhead home, Miss Carpenter wore thick-lensed glasses and would sometimes focus on you a baleful glare, head on one side, and come out with some cutting personal observation like "You have an ugly neck". Mostly she was obsessed with herself. Once when I had answered the front door to find her there after a long absence, she had turned her back, cocked her head and breathed urgently, "Don't say anything. Don't talk. I can't think of anything but that blackbird. Listen." But it was the study of freshwater fish that kept her from despair.

We had heard of Chamberlain's announcement that Britain was in a state of war with Germany from a man in Lorne Road leaning over his gate in his shirtsleeves on our trek back from Divine Service at Park Grove Strict and Particular Baptist

Chapel. My parents were Calvinists who had inherited their parents' belief that only a predestined Elect would go to Heaven, that every word of the Bible was literally true, that Sunday was the Sabbath Day to be kept holy, that the theatre, cinema and even radio were devices of the Devil, and that sex was something that didn't bear talking about.

At school, ever since at the age of seven I had told them that Miss Ross had pronounced the parting of the Red Sea a natural phenomenon, I had been barred from Scripture lessons. I had to sit at the back of other classes, a fish out of water. One year my predicament was overlooked. I didn't like to remind anyone and I spent the weekly period lurking in the cloakroom, pretending to be looking for something in my locker or macintosh pocket when anyone passed through.

One winter afternoon when I was fifteen I went down town to the Plaza Cinema and for some time walked up and down in the slush outside, glancing at the stills and the dimly-lit carpeted foyer as though they were inducements to the Bottomless Pit. After a while I walked another mile or so to the Roxy. There were pictures of high-kicking chorus girls and I proceeded to the Scala where I gave God a third chance to divert me, before it was too late, from the primrose path. Sleet was falling and a gust of warm air, smelling of sickly-sweet disinfect-ant, enveloped me as a couple of boys shoved nonchalantly through the swing doors. I went in. It was a Will Hay film and I couldn't help laughing.

Going to chapel meant a half-hour's walk (no bus-riding on Sunday) from the leafy suburbs through a seedy district of terraced houses and tenements, where what we called 'street arabs' ran wild and barefoot. The chapel was a converted Dames' school at the end of a countryfied lane, completely hidden from the outside world by high walls and an apple orchard. The glass of the windows was frosted and ribbed and through it the apple-boughs stirred in a breeze like fronds in an ocean's depths. That bottle-green blur was the background to many a desperate childhood fantasy as the voice droned on ("And here there are five points we have to consider . . . ") and time crawled on leaden ticks of a wall-clock that had had its chime taken out.

2

Sometimes, in desperation, the two younger sisters and I, who formed a middle 'clique' in our family of seven, would fashion nodding, gesticulating figures out of knotted handker-chiefs and have to let out the painfully-suppressed laughter in bursts of breathy coughing that only made things funnier. Miss Sloane, who sat with her brother in the pew in front of us and had a genuine cough of her own, would look round accusingly as though we were mocking her. She was a wizened little dressmaker who had once made me a flannel dressing-gown that smelt of fish. We were fascinated by the way she would manoeuvre a cough-sweet out of her handbag under cover of a handkerchief and inch it up her flat bosom to her mouth as though to have popped it in quite openly would have been an affront to God. After one service, in the lane where the meagre congregation would gather after the service for an exchange of heavy salutations, Mr Sloane had said, "Well, you've got to get your life over with, haven't you?"

My father, who was secretary of a shipping company and ruled us with a firm but loving hand, alternated most Sundays at the desk under the pulpit with Mr Shaw, an elderly postman with a limp and glasses that slipped to the end of his long nose. He prepared his sermons on Saturday nights in his study, where rows of massive Concordances crowded shelves next to box-files containing bills and receipts and school reports and where there was a cane, not often used, tucked away behind a cupboard. His sermons were at least of reasonable length and lucidity. Mr Shaw read haltingly and interminably from the collected sermons of Mr Philpot or Mr Popham and his prayers would sinuously fasten on himself as the most miserable of sinners. His voice would choke and there would be a painful silence before he could get out a simile like 'worthless worm'.

The pulpit was reserved for visiting preachers from other Strict and Particular Baptist chapels in the north. Their idiosyncrasies provided rich material for our game of 'Chapel' in the breakfast-room at home, with a pulpit on the table and a congregation usually consisting of Aunt Alice, sitting ramrod straight and severe, Great Uncle Jim jerking himself in the nick of time from sleep, Mr Shaw drooping his head in despair and wiping away many a tear, and Miss Sloane getting at a cough-sweet. Rachel was particularly good at Mr Caton who had an extraordinary way of mouthing his words as though chewing cud. On some words his jaw would seem temporarily to get stuck.

But in more recent years the minutely familiar interior of Park Grove had been the setting for a seemingly unresolvable spiritual conflict between a straitlaced inherited faith and a vaguely formulated credo that had its roots in literature, music, paintings, the English countryside, the imagined past and, increasingly, a search, half-mystical, half-lustful, for That Not Impossible She. Nothing less than a sign or a voice from Heaven would now do. And it would need to be a good deal more conclusive than the kind of experiences related by Aunt Grace in a long and earnest correspondence, like being 'given strength' to face her first needlework class. It would need to be more like what happened to St Paul on the road to Damascus or what had soured the fruits of evil so manifestly enjoyed by St Augustine and John Donne.

On this first Sunday of the war I was 23 days from being 20, introverted, immature, looking back to childhood as to a Golden Age and to the future with apprehension. At Birkenhead School, in the wake of an elder brother who had 'carried all before him', I had distinguished myself in nothing except the number of prizes I had taken away from Speech Day platforms. But I was not up to scholarship standard (my brother had won an exhibition to Magdalen, Oxford) and at 17, with no clear idea what I wanted to be, had gone for an interview at the Public Schools Careers Bureau in London. A Captain Pullein-Thompson had looked at me sourly when I expressed a vague interest in publishing and journalism. "I suppose you were good at English," he growled and a door seemed to clang. He got me a job with a Liverpool produce merchant which specialized in hams and dog food and offered 'excellent chances of promotion'.

I lasted nearly a year at Morrell's, pacing morning and evening the open deck of the Woodside/Pierhead ferryboat with determined-looking businessmen in bowlers (as my father had done for the past twenty-five years) and wondering if I could ever become the Average Man. I was started on the bottom rung of the ladder, wrapping up advertising displays and sample tins of Red Heart dog food and staggering with them to the Post Office, delivering invoices and cheques to offices and dock warehouses, and taking round the afternoon tea.

The other lads called me Hunkus of the Mohicans and forgave me my public school accent when I became adept at filching biscuits when Mrs Hoare's back was turned at the tea-urn, and when it leaked out that, instead of taking all the mail round by hand, I had been posting those with addresses at some distance from the office and spending an hour or so in the Kardomah, reading. When I left they presented me, over a farewell drink, with a nine-stanza poem:

> ' . . . Around the City he will roam
> In his feathers bright and red.
> "Why should I trudge this filthy snow?
> I'll post them all instead."
>
> And so to a café he will go,
> And sit him down to read
> Those classics that he loves so much,
> To trash he pays no heed.'

I had got a job on the bi-weekly *Birkenhead News*, whose editor was an Old Boy, and was soon busy writing up council meetings, police court cases, Conservative fêtes, learning the appropriate phrase at the side of the open coffin in a terrace-house parlour where lay the late president of the local bowling club, getting a lift back in Mr Ball's hearse from some arctic cemetery after collecting the names of the mourners ("*My* name! I'm the Deputy Town Clerk!"), posing as art and music critics because no one else was interested and trying to eschew phrases like "Miss Tostle was adequate at the piano".

I had signed an agreement as impressive-looking as Magna Carta, which bound me to a three-year apprenticeship, earning five shillings a week the first year, ten the second and a pound the third. The only direct instruction I remember receiving was to write copy sideways on the pad, not lengthwise.

Now war was here and the blue sky above the hawthorn and laburnum stretched wide open to Germany. The cucumber sandwiches were finished and the animal food expert was looking restive. His son's fiancée was pretty in a mousy way, with bare brown legs that she nervously smoothed, but shyness was not a bond I looked for in a Not Impossible She. Mystery, yes, a certain elusiveness ("Oh stay and hear thy true love's calling") but not that clammy disease called shyness.

My father stood up and Kathleen Carpenter reached for her bag on the grass. Then she leaned back again in her chair and that sour, searching look of hers flickered from face to face. Her eyes caught mine and fastened there and her lips, on which even a smile sat like a sneer, twitched. "And what are *you* going to do about it all?" she asked, rhetorically.

CHAPTER TWO

Next evening, as recorded in the 'Diary in Wartime' I had just started, I attended a meeting of potential Conscientious Objectors and wondered if God had ordained that it should be held in the drawing-room of 35 Chestnut Grove, Higher Tranmere. For this Victorian stone house on the other side of the town, now owned by Quakers, had for long been the home of my Scottish-born maternal grandparents; here I had been born and here were enshrined my earliest memories.

It was a nondescript collection of people, including Duncan, a sixth form friend with whom I shared artistic endeavours (self-taught piano playing, dabbling with pastel and paint, verse-writing), a taste for surreal humour (e.g. the Marx brothers, Edward Lear) and an anti-establishment bias. For me leanings towards pacifism had originated in a school expedition to Germany, in 1936, which took in the desolate battlefields and eerie forts of Verdun. I had since been haunted by imaginings of the Western Front, finding in the writings of Siegfried Sassoon, Robert Graves, Wilfred Owen, Erich Remarque, a fascination hard to resist. I felt how, once experienced, the huddled horror of the trenches, the nightmare No Man's Land, might draw one hypnotically back from the shallow comforts of Blighty: the monstrous anger of the guns a Sirens' song. You would be back There.

Only two days before, I had received a long letter from my brother Martin in Oxford in which he presented a reasoned analysis of the various arguments for pacifism, and proceeded to demolish both them and the mixed-up case I had put to him. At school I had gone so far as confronting my father with a request to leave the Officers' Training Corps and join the class disparagingly called 'Remnants', where the time was filled with non-curricula subjects like art and natural history. There had been a pained refusal to contemplate my opting out of this character-forming activity, and, from my mother, a relevant Scriptural text on my pillow that night.

I had to admit that there was no real moral basis to my aversion to the Corps. I merely hated the way that the donning of khaki could change an individual into a shouted number, a manipulated puppet. "Heft ... heft ... heft, right, heft ... in *step* there!" Sgt-Major C.N. Jones would snarl out of the corner of his mouth as we snaked on an Armistice Day parade through the streets of the town behind the blaring band, the tubby Housemaster and Classical Sixth Latin master transformed at our head into Captain Williamson, strutting, naked sword pointed to heaven. "Heft ... heft ... Put some *swank* into it!"

Charlie Jones, who also took Gym, had an automatic antipathy for anyone on the Classics side, and, indeed, for most book-learning ("What's the good of knowledge? It's wisdom you want.") and shared the disgust of Old Boy faithfuls when, under the editorship of my brother, the school magazine changed from a stereotyped record of mostly sporting events into an outlet for iconoclasts, versifiers who had read Yeats and T.S. Eliot, photographers focusing on subjects far more esoteric than the First Fifteen.

One Thursday afternoon, making a preliminary inspection of the Corps formed up in the Quad, he singled out one of my buttons as being tarnished and ordered me to report forthwith to the Company Commander. Snapping to attention in front of my brother, who stood rigidly facing the assembled Corps, was the severest test of the mutual non-recognition that we adhered to when at school. It was satisfying in my last year, as art editor of the *Birkonian*, to produce a sketch for the OTC Notes of a grinning cadet with lank hair sprouting from his cap, buttons and puttees undone, butt of rifle on shoulder, saluting with arm outstretched, though by then I had learned that Charlie had a mordant sense of humour and enjoyed nothing more than a slanging-match.

It was hard to gauge how far pacifism now appealed as a

reflex to those dragooned, khaki-drab Thursday afternoons, and the sweltering purgatory of two 1935 weeks under canvas at Aldershot, in an aura less of rivalry with other public schools as of an overwhelming conformity, a mass display of blind obedience under the banner 'More swank!'

But now, listening to the talk in the Chestnut Grove drawing-room, I began to feel that there was another kind of arrogance in the assumption that the vast majority of the community was sleep-marching to the sound of the guns, and we enlightened few were entitled to opt out and see them go. One could respect the Quaker, who would offer his services to an ambulance unit, but most, like me, hid the flabbiness of our convictions under a smoke-screen of non-conformist clichés.

The house stirred memories of a time when one did not see as through a glass darkly, but, with delight or wonder, face to face. Here had sat my grandfather, white-bearded beneath his lower lip, a patriarch whose word was law. John Knox as much as Calvin had been his inspiration and he would turn begging nuns from the door as envoys of the Whore of Babylon. But the stories of his Scottish childhood that had come down to us were lit with humour and pleasure in at least some of the senses.

This room had seen that first remembered Christmas party, and up those stairs, across the landing, in the big front bedroom, I had first met Death. I was five and can only conjecture that there had been a gathering of the clans by a vague memory of many hushed voices. More clearly I can recall being taken upstairs by Aunt Jane and Aunt Grace and being afraid as one of them turned the knob of the bedroom door.

The blinds must have been drawn because I remember the dimness of light and then being lifted up beside the great double bed. Last time I had been here I had watched as Grandma had hauled herself into a sitting position among the pillows by a tasselled cord tied to the brass-knobbed rail at the foot of the bed. What I now saw was a Thing, not a person. The face under the lace cap had a putty nose, smoothed sea-shells for eyelids, lips pale as string.

"Grandma's in Heaven," whispered one of the Aunts in that special Chapel voice, and my hand was reached out to touch the corrugated brow. It was marble-cold and I recoiled. "She's happy now for always and always."

It was on 6 November that I went for my medical at the Territorial Drill Hall. I had finally come to the conclusion that I had no valid case for registering as a conscientious objector, and the only unresolved question was whether I should opt for the Navy or Air Force, both of which suggested a less regimented life than the Army. I was accompanied by a reporter from the rival *Birkenhead Advertiser*, who had a limp and faulty vision and commiserated with me on the forthcoming fettered life he was to escape.

The last of the examining doctors asked if I had had any special complaints or illnesses and I mentioned chickenpox and the asthma I had occasionally suffered as a boy. Some nights had been a prolonged fight for breath, propped up in an armchair, trying to inhale the spluttering fumes of Potter's Asthma Cure. I was sent back to the doctor who checked breathing and he put me through more rigorous tests.

In the final booth the Chairman briskly completed the form, handed it to me and said, "You will not be required." It was an insignificant-looking buff certificate, on one side, "Description of Man: Age 20, height 5 ft 9½ins, colour of eyes, blue-grey, colour of hair, L' Brown", on the other, name and address, and, in red ink, 'Grade – III (three)'.

The *Advertiser* reporter had been passed Grade II and was as incredulous as I. An initial feeling of elation, of being let off a prison sentence, was followed by a stunned realization of the chairman's curt 'not required'. Like lame Willie who saw all the other children trooping behind the Pied Piper into the mountainside, I was outside. However the tide of war flowed, I would never be There.

Six months later, the Low Countries overrun, the Germans at last up against the British and French armies, Anthony Eden, as War Minister, made a radio appeal to men between 17 and 65 who had 'no other commitments' to become Local Defence Volunteers. So it was back to khaki of a kind again, with evening drill in the school quad and round the cricket pitch, shooting practice at the range, lectures by First War veterans attempting to dispel the feeling that it was all a bit of a charade.

But there was a certain sense of exhilaration about those early days in the Home Guard. We were as raggle-taggle an assortment as any that stood by for the Armada or Napoleon, inadequately trained, inadequately armed, but it did seem after Dunkirk that we might be called upon to make some kind of desperate last-ditch stand.

There was, indeed, a night in September, 1940, when the telephone rang at home with an urgent message to report for duty. Our local headquarters was a requisitioned house at the top of our road opposite the cricket ground and there senior officers were conferring and prodding maps in a purposeful way. There had been a nationwide alert that the invasion might be on its way, with prospects of parachute drops just about anywhere.

It was not a ditch in which my squad was called upon to make our stand but a disused rubbish dump in a field that sloped down to a stream called the Fender and the one-track railway that meandered across the Wirral and into North Wales. The line had constituted one of our more aimless patrols, clumping in the darkness from sleeper to sleeper, flashing dimmed torches through tunnels and down embankments. As a target for saboteurs it could hardly have figured prominently on Hitler's maps.

In childhood the railway had been the most romantic of all fantasy worlds. We would picnic close to it by a footbridge over the Fender in real country, with daisies, buttercups and thistles, reedy tadpole ponds, larks whirring into the blue, fly-covered cowpats and cows themselves, breathing menace. The supreme thrill came when, far down the curving line, appeared a wisp of white smoke and distantly came the whistle and chug of an approaching train.

The game was to wait until it snaked just into sight and then make a mad dash between the thistles and cowpats, over the steep wooden stile, up the echoing stone steps of the iron bridge, and then to be tiptoe against the balustrade as the belching engine went under. There might be a glimpse of the engine-driver leaning from his cabin and then the tops of the carriages flowing under your feet. Watching it receding across the buttercup meadows into a distance that beckoned to Wales was to feel a yearning that could not be put into words.

From the rubbish-dump it was invisible over invisible fields in the dark, wet, early morning hours. Leaning or crouching among the rotted garbage and rusted tins, we kept our loaded rifles under our capes, wondering what we would do if anything happened. Not until dawn seeped in and we saw each other materialize, drenched and shivering, with the rain swilling from our helmets, did the ludicrousness of the situation fully register.

From the outset of the war fear of air raids had been at the back of everybody's mind. Though unaware of the Air Ministry's nightmare calculations of 600,000 dead and 1,200,000 injured in the first sixty days, and of the stockpiles of cardboard and papier mâché coffins awaiting, we had been keyed up to unimaginable horrors, not least by those terrible scenes of London's destruction in the recently distributed film version of H.G. Wells' *The Shape of Things to Come.*

When the first air raid sirens wailed over Merseyside I was on Home Guard drill on the cricket ground, and with little hesitation we cantered for the New School buildings. The basement boiler-room was locked and we decided the safest place would be the cloakrooms, with less exposure there to flying glass.

One or two of the ultra-cautious who had india-rubbers in their pockets, tentatively bit onto them. (The theory was that if the mouth was kept partly open there would be less danger of bomb-blast blowing out your ear-drums.) One man got under a heavy trestle table but came out after a time when nobody else followed.

It was a lovely evening, not a cloud in the sky. We strained our ears but there was no indication of anything else being there either. After a while we sauntered to the door and into the open, glancing up at the idly-floating balloons. A solitary RAF plane, off course, had flown over, very high, we learned later.

When I got home I found that the family had shut themselves in the basement, gas-masks to hand, cotton-wool in ears as well as rubbers in mouths. Muff, our ageing cat, had been put in the big old copper in the scullery, where Rose the charlady had once

12

boiled the weekly wash, and the heavy wooden lid put on it so as to let in only a chink of air.

It was not until the spring of 1941 that the blitz came to Merseyside. I had by then bade an unreluctant farewell to the *Birkenhead News* to become a reporter in the Liverpool office of the *Manchester Daily Despatch*. On night duties the Press Club, on the second floor of a Victorian building in Lime Street, was the rendezvous for a handful of reporters and a pack of hearty, boozily-Philistine associate members – alderman, lawyer, cinema manager, dentist, restaurateur.

A drunken chorus heralded the first raid. Birkenhead, we soon learned, was bearing the brunt. Only Mother, Barbara and Geoffrey were at home (my father at a board meeting in London, Martin now in the army in India, Cathie in the WAAF, Rachel and Mildred in the Land Army). The line was dead when I phoned. With the Mersey mine-infested, it was not until 6 that I caught the first underground train. In Oxton a land-mine had landed near St Saviour's church. Sunrise coloured crumbled mounds that had been houses known from childhood. I hurried for the first glimpse of home. The pillar-box, the swoop of Beresford Road, hawthorn and laburnum – it stood.

Shattered sheets of glass glittered on the front lawn. Soot coated the dining-room. I clumped down the steep steps to the basement. Around three camp chairs in the kitchen rugs and cushions lay discarded. My portable radio stood on the table beside an open Bible. In previous 'nuisance' raids Mother had a way of frowning at outbursts of hilarity that came as a reflex to the pounding of nearby ack-ack guns. "Be solemn," she would say, tightening away the smile trembling on her own lips. I ran up to her room. She was awake but quite matter-of-fact about it all.

The raid was the prelude to the full-blooded Blitz in May, Merseyside's 'turn'. On the second night, directing stirrup-pumps on to the roof of the fish-market alight below, we in the Press Club seemed encircled by fire. Buildings in every direction belched smoke and flame, the sky streamed with sparks and balls of fire which bounced from roofs, showering the streets. Walking the streets later – Lewis's an inferno, explosions

13

underscoring the steady roar and crackle, a burst water-main gushing blood-red, firemen around Blackler's leaping from avalanches of blazing masonry, Cooper's wall alight, Horne Brothers flickering, the Bluecoat Chambers sprouting tendrils, every corner opening on a new flamescape – gave an awful feeling of exhilaration. "The fucking bastards!" my companion kept repeating. "Aren't they fucking bastards!"

Chaos continued daily. Hoses snaked from the docks but many fire engines, from as far as Blackpool, stood helplessly by. Transport was confined to lorries (in all that smoke cigarettes were at a premium); Army telephone wires linked control centres. Long before dark the trek to the shelters and under-ground stations began. After the All Clear, crowds gathered around the new outbreaks, connoisseurs of conflagrations. "That's nothing. You should have seen . . . "

With telephone communications in Liverpool disrupted, I got lifts through the Mersey Tunnel to phone Manchester with reports inadequate even by censorship standards. Daytime meant a gruesome prowl of newly-bombed residential districts for 'human stories'. 'Liverpool licking its wounds' became the cliché, and soon the Press Club regulars stood smugly esconced as before behind their whiskies and Family Ales, a little more vociferous than before about what *they* would do to the Hun.

Three months later the diary gives a good deal more space to a holiday in London than to the Liverpool blitz, largely because of Molly. Molly lived at Hayward's Heath, worked in a City bank, had met my sister Mildred on a French course at Eastbourne and I had been reading between the lines of a lengthy correspondence with her for some months past. In a snapshot she had looked pretty in a tennis-skirt, holding a racket and smiling enigmatically.

I had arranged to be carrying the Penguin *Ariel*, André Maurois' biography of Shelley, outside the National Gallery at 12.30. And there she was. We went straight in to the crowded concert hall where Myra Hess was giving the five-hundredth lunch-hour recital, and stole glances at each other through the Appassionata Sonata and Jesu, Joy of Man's Desiring.

Over lunch at the Corner House, the diary records, she was

seen to be "smallish, firm, compact, dark curls curved over a grey hat. Her face is round, pale, grey-green eyes with dark lids, snub nose, pouting, melancholy lips: her voice low, musical, hesitant, often accompanied by the raising of an eyebrow over an eye of weak sight: her smile, upper lip curved upwards, very charming. Her letters suggested bounce and breathlessness: instead she was cool, self-contained, almost evasive."

We saw *The Taming of the Shrew* at the Regent's Park Open Air Theatre, Henry Moore's tube-shelterers at the National Gallery, joined a queue circling right round the Albert Hall to hear Beethoven at the Proms. On the second day we heard Schubert at the National Gallery, after lunch walked and sat around the Serpentine, a day of hot sunshine and welcome tree-shade, talking of this and that – "a smoke-screen of conversation over the insistence of the senses".

At Victoria Station that night "in the faintly-lit gloom her face was very pale, her eyes gleamed darkly – a pale, dark-centred flower. We said we had been glad to meet each other – her train was in – we shook hands and I went without looking back. I sat in the buffet, ate sausages, drank a bitter, feeling remote from all the people there, on an island of enchantment, melancholy enchantment."

It was an enchantment I only just kept alive until our final meeting a year later through a bombardment of letters no less bouncy or breathless and the birthday gift of her 'first poem for two years'. It was called 'Sunset over the Hills' and was written in the train to Victoria from Hayward's Heath.

"I stood and watched the hills from whence I came,
The sun was sinking in a pool of blood,
O'erhead the sky, be-spattered with his shame,
Hung, dripping, in a multi-coloured flood."

By the calendar, 14 March, 1942, was the first day of Spring, for me a turning-point. In my room my bags were packed, labelled 'Grasmere', Holland Road, Chorlton-cum-Hardy, Manchester. Though working for the Manchester office of the *Daily Despatch* would take me only fifty miles from home, it was my first uprooting and I felt a trip down Memory Lane was indicated.

On the cricket ground the shadows of the great beeches were beginning to stretch out, and a golden glow suffused the Tudor-Gothic of the old school buildings – clock tower, classrooms and assembly hall, boarding house, chapel, gymnasium. A nostalgic glow, too, could just about be conjured up in a backward look at the ten long years when I had been part of it all.

On the debit side, thanks to our upbringing, had been the underlying feeling, shared in varying degrees by my brothers and sisters, of being different, set apart. My first intimation of this came when, at the age of seven, I was picked for a fairly leading role, as a mouse, in the Prep School's Christmas play to be staged in Big School, only to have my excitement dashed by parental edict. My mouse's costume, with others in the play, was being hired, they had learned, from the firm that supplied costumes to the Liverpool Playhouse and other such dens of iniquity, and was thereby ruled out. Instead I was fitted out by nimble-fingered Aunt Lizzie as a Christmas card. Sporting illustrated squares of cardboard back and front, like a sandwich man, all I had to do was to rotate slowly across the stage from one wing to the other, and disappear. Ashcroft played the mouse.

On the credit side was the effect of the grounding we had been given in the King James Bible, large chunks of which our father set us to memorize for the afternoon Sunday school he presided over in the drawing-room in our earlier years. Not as the holy word of God, but as an anthology of matchless prose and poetry, it was to make English literature my favourite subject and the imagined past an endless fascination.

By great good fortune the Senior School English master, Gerald Claypole, was the one master in the school I whole-heartedly admired. A charismatic character, his had been the inspiration behind the new-look school magazine, and it was he who breathed life on the annual school play.

The first two plays I ever saw, his productions of *Macbeth* and *Twelfth Night,* were occasions of such magic as almost to make worthwhile the deprivations that had gone before. From the moment the lights dimmed in Big School, the velvet curtains swished apart and the First Witch's "When shall we three meet again?" rose above the metallic claps of thunder, I was in thrall to Shakespeare.

Re-enacting scenes at home that Christmas, I tried to imagine myself as participant rather than spectator, and wondered how different things might have been if my parents had been as other parents, and, nine years ago, I, not Ashcroft, had taken a bow in that mouse's hired costume.

CHAPTER THREE

'Grasmere', a drab house in a drab road in a suburb of a drab city, proved to be a boarding-house for eccentric journalists run by a motherly witch. Life there was unreal, unpredictable, sometimes hilarious and made nine months of humdrum reporting at Kemsley House quite bearable.

Mrs Leighton was alone in the house the night I arrived. I deposited my bags in what had been the front drawing-room, full of heavy furniture and arty ornaments, with a couch bed down the middle, and joined her in a small, bright kitchen where a fire burned in an old-fashioned range. She was a Gloucestershire woman, with apple-cheeks, a fuzz of dark springy hair and two protruding front teeth that fought a constant and losing battle to get tucked in behind her lower lip.

As she prepared supper she talked in what I was later to learn was her special voice reserved for new acquaintances. It was soon made clear that she was not accustomed to this kind of life but that she had made an exception for newspaper Boys because her husband, a sub-editor on the *Daily Herald*, was one. They were childless and the Boys were like a family to her, a big happy family.

I answered her questions about myself as impressively as possible and her bright, darting eyes registered approval. One of her closest friends, she said, was a very wealthy lady who lived in Didsbury and had uncanny powers of seeing into the future. She was very interested herself in the occult though her husband Bill said it was all a lot of nonsense. He was a funny old thing, but she knew I would like him. She'd had plenty of suitors before she married him. Once on the beach at Lyme Regis an Admiral's son had tried to kiss her. He shouldn't have, but he was really very nice.

She liked artistic things; I'd probably noticed the engravings on the stairs; they were insured for £50. My room had some very nice things, too. She collected old furniture and objects dart. Bill didn't really appreciate things like that. He was a funny old thing but she knew I'd like him. As it was Saturday night he was at a pub in Didsbury with a couple of the Boys. It was a nice, select pub, nothing common. Perhaps I'd like to join them after supper.

We found them seated in the corner of a smoky, noisy saloon. Bill was sitting in indulgent silence as the others argued the merits of Moiseiwitsch. He was a heavy, placid Yorkshireman, slow-talking and slow-thinking, cheese to his wife's chalk. After initial pleasantries the conversation reverted to Moiseiwitsch, thence to the ideal Cleopatra. The London critics had been having a field-day with a heavily accented Russian actress playing the part in the West End. "*O weedered ee de garland o de var . . .* " Lubricated by old ale, the declamations flowed. I marvelled that Manchester had produced in two hours what Liverpool had, with a few exceptions, failed to produce in a year.

My four fellow-lodgers proved, indeed, to be stimulating companions. Clifford Speight was Mrs Leighton's ideal of a 'gentleman', cultured, fastidious, usually gracious. He had moods of silence, reading in his room or in the back garden hammock, plodding through Chopin on the ramshackle dining-room upright, escaping for walks. In his cups he was devil-may-care, telling coarse stories no one appreciated more than himself. His laughter, high-pitched and prolonged, had a life of its own. Over lunch one day, hearing Mrs Leighton's witch-like guffaw erupt in the kitchen, he turned to Bill. "I do think your wife's repulsive," he said, "Oh, she is repulsive!" and went off into peels, the two separated laughters mingling like a descant.

Mac, who worked in the Art Department of the *Daily Express*, was regarded as a bit of an odd bird. He concealed shyness under a cloak of brusqueness, and, though his dead-pan expression could break into a smile of great charm, he held intimacies at arm's length. I warmed to him on the first morning when, after cooking his own breakfast of kidney and bacon, he butted in

19

on the Beethoven sonata I was trying to coax from the piano to ask, without introduction, "Do you walk?"

We set off at an Olympic pace, Mac erect, head back, thick-lensed spectacles glinting in the sun, swinging his arms like a guardsman. Long, lonely walks, whatever the weather, were a morning ritual and he spent holidays tramping his native Yorkshire moors. As we swung through the suburbs of Chorlton-cum-Hardy, he began to point out the small landmarks that had taken his fancy – a Gothic lodge, a pepper-pot church, the limestone ornamentation of Longford Park, an industrial skyline. "I find them amusing. Don't let them get you down."

Mac was a great source of worry to Mrs Leighton. He repulsed all her motherly advances. She liked to wave her Boys off to work and it was a recognized ritual that we wave back to her, as she stood in the doorway, from the corner across the road. Mac had early on put a stop to that nonsense by keeping to the shelter of the garden wall, not crossing the road, but taking a wide detour to the bus stop. "I wonder how long she stood there looking at that corner," he mused with satisfaction.

Mac regarded as his masterstroke the way he had dealt with her suspected habit of reading any postcards that came in the post as well as any letters left lying around. Strange cards began to arrive for him. A sepia photograph of the Hotel de Ville at Boulogne, one of its windows marked in ink with a cross, and on the back the one word: "Remember?" A reproduction of Paul Nash's "The Empty Room": "Let this picture speak for me." An ordinary postcard reading "Things cannot go on like this. I must know one way or the other. Lou." Another picture of the Hotel de Ville at Boulogne with an anonymous message: *"Je t'adore."*

For Mrs Leighton, who liked nothing better than to share a confidence, it must have been a cruel ordeal to have to keep her lips tight on Mac's incredible double life. The postmarks were in different parts of England, and for us the intriguing mystery was the identity of the 'friends' Mac had casually mentioned as having entered into the conspiracy.

'Grasmere' revolved around indefatigable, irrepressible, exhausting Hilda Leighton. Though different work-shifts meant that she was serving breakfast in the kitchen for one while others trooped back from the local pub for lunch in the dining-room, she never wilted. She took Bill's moods in her stride. Swaying back from a late session at the Press Club, he would sink into a chair by the kitchen fire, exuding benevolence. 'Silly cuckoo' he would mumble as she loosened his tie, got him into his cardigan and bedroom slippers, coaxed him to eat and finally to bed.

Next morning, unshaven and bleary-eyed in the same chair, he would launch into a blow-by-blow account of yet another 'bit of a do'. Drinking for Bill was a real bout. Somebody would 'sling out' a pint, it would be 'knocked back', another would be 'whipped out', they kept on 'coming up'. "It's the water-waggon for me, my boy," he would say, fairly oozing remorse.

Later you would see him in the drab back garden, slowly pacing the lawn, crouching over a wilting plant and lifting its head, peering over the wall at the hen-run where the three chicks his neighbour had bought at a market had turned out to be indubitable cocks, tapping the tortoise, looking broodingly back at the house as he relit his pipe. "You know," he told me once in the Press Club, talking of twenty years of childless marriage with Hilda, "she thinks the world of me."

Withy Grove was a great barn of a place, the largest newspaper office in Europe. The *Daily Despatch* news staff shared a huge untidy room with the *Evening Chronicle*, eight of us sitting round a long table with the News Editor at the top, dishing out stories like a father carving the joint. My first was a concert at Bellevue where 5,000 people heard a special arrangement of Beethoven's Fifth Symphony for massed bands and choirs and I was able to report that never could Fate have knocked more loudly on the door. My second was at Oldham where three Nazis had escaped after riots at a prisoner-of-war camp. Three hundred Germans were marched through the streets to the station to be transferred elsewhere – soldiers, airmen, U-boat and merchant navy crews. "Don't they look ordinary?" said one of the mill-girls who had poured out to gape.

Most stories were worked up on the office telephone and it took something like a murder to get one far afield. Few of them seemed worthy of a diary mention. An exception, no doubt because of its inward-looking implications, was a night at the Midlands Hotel for a press launching of a repertory season of Noel Coward plays.

A private suite with trolley-loads of drinks and snacks and two waiters had been provided for the reception, arranged by Richard Clowes, a theatre press agent, with whom I had had a long session in Liverpool after an Emlyn Williams premiere. (He had found me 'interesting' and suggested I was wasting my time in the provinces.) He looked a little worried when, after half an hour, there was still only myself, a woman from the *News Chronicle*, the Opera House manager and Judy Campbell, the leading lady, present. But Noel Coward's urbanity did not desert him when he at last made a dramatic entrance to what was scheduled to have been a babel of chatter and laughter and clouds of cigarette smoke, to find our little huddle.

He was my first real celebrity and I was tongue-tied at first as he swept through a series of polished anecdotes about past Mancunian experiences. At one stage, in full flow, he turned on me a sudden aside: "Don't laugh. It might hurt." But after a few more drinks I got in on the act and was soon swopping ideas with him as to how a British-produced epic about the American Civil War could be made corny and patronizing enough to challenge *Mrs Miniver*, Hollywood's current version of Britain taking it. "Come and tell me what you think of the new play," he said before leaving.

"I knew something would come of that tête-à-tête," Clowes said. I told him I thought Coward an egomaniac. "You're a terribly severe young man," he replied. "At present you're shy and I can see you becoming just as much an egomaniac." Down in the reception hall he suddenly said, "You really are an extraordinary person. What are you really like? What do you want?" I was saved from having to reply by the arrival of the Opera House manager. We all went to a nearby pub and drank beer.

After a number of beers on top of the gins and limes, I walked unsteadily back to the office in a pleasant haze. It was very gratifying to be thought mysterious and worth analysing. The news room was deserted except for the late man. After a long struggle with the elusive keys of my typewriter, I pocketed what

I had written and phoned for a taxi. Next morning I read: "Two new Noel Corrd plays wull be shown in a fotnigh's repertry at the opra house, Manchessert, The experiment wull be so succ3full thut the whole compant wull be in rapturesa there will be no Bomonbay willpsoury woiOuns why. e   d."

There were occasional air raids but the active war was something you read about in the papers or heard on the News, with Stuart Hibberd or Alvar Liddell reading it. When Churchill spoke to the nation, wireless sets were ringed by expectant faces, waiting for the bulldog growl, the intimations of progress or setbacks that seemed reassuring alike in that gruff, sing-song, unemotional voice, the cocking of a snook that would give us a new catchphrase to smugly bandy about – "Some chicken – some neck!", "Italian guttersnipe . . . ", "Mr . . . er . . . Schickelgruber . . . " Crowding around the office radio the night he announced Russia's entry into the war, we were more intrigued as to how he would verbally surmount this tricky ideological hurdle than about the history-making implications of the alliance.

By now it was hard to recall the days before blackout and dimmed headlights, rationing and salvage drives, roads and railways ostensibly leading from nowhere to nowhere, reminders that journeys should be really necessary and that careless talk cost lives. But underneath it all life had not fundamentally changed.

I spent Whit weekend at Blackpool, writing about the influx of holidaymakers who had found this journey as necessary as it had been in peacetime, and kept a copy of an account of it I wrote in one of my occasional, morale-boosting letters to Duncan, whose latest letter, from an Army posting in Scotland, had pictured him, on guard duty in the bleak early hours, passing the time by "humming the first and second subjects of each movement of every symphony I know."

"I stayed three nights in a private hotel on the South Promenade, where a huge Lancashire woman sat surfeited after meals, staring cow-like into the empty grate: all the other occupants were Lancashire, bah goom, full of pompous platitudes: 'Ay, we're all growing older, lad . . . '

"The tripper's Blackpool comes to the surface on the central promenade with its orgy of fun fairs, oyster stalls, waxworks, slot machines, weighing machines, deformities, enormities.

" 'Come and see' intoned one loudspeaker voice 'the greatest work of art the world has ever seen. Jacob Epstein's Jacob and the Angel. God versus Man, three and a half tons of Derbyshire alabaster, worth its weight in pure gold. It's sensational, it's symbolical, it's diabolical and every other -olical. It will make you think, it will make you talk, it will probably make you weep. Three and a half tons of alabaster. Come and see.'

"I went. Jacob and the Angel were wrestling in a sand-pit stuck all over with cactus plants, lit with pink and blue spotlights. Between the legs of the Angel a mirror was tilted which reflected, if not credit on the exhibitors, a clear view of Jacob's private parts. Customers were very shy of looking at the World's Greatest Work of Art: they examined embroidered robes worn by Pope Pius the Ninth, photographs of film stars (Mae West in the arena with God versus Man), they examined each other, finally their eyes fluttered like timid butterflies over this breathless heap of alabaster. It was then that a plain, scared-looking girl sidled up: 'I don't know if you're acquainted with the story of Jacob and the Angel . . . ' And, after a bit, 'Of course Epstein's work is very difficult to understand at first . . . '

"That is one side of Blackpool. Wander through side streets, past pubs, fish-and-chip shops, displays of crude postcards (bottoms and booze, lavatories and lust) and you come to streets of lodging houses now chock-a-block with the RAF. In the evening every window shows a tableau: four airmen playing cards, an airman playing the piano, an airman reading the paper, an airman writing home – a desolating sight, while landladies' daughters glance over their knitting or magazine, hoping for the Hollywood miracle.

"Lustier airmen and lustier girls are gallivanting on the promenade, waiting for dusk and the nightly hug, by sea-wall or bus shelter. When it comes, they lie dark shapes in the sand, kissing, breaking away, kissing again, instruments of an imperative desire. Certainly this is no place to bring illusions of love – mystic, sublime or merely 'romantic'. "

24

In Wordsworth country there was escapism of another kind. I had been to Barrow-in-Furness, where ship-welders were clamouring for extra clothing coupons, broke my journey at Grange-over-Sands and climbed to a hilltop.

"To the West the estuary sparkled silver, east the mountains of Lakeland rose to peaks capped with snow. I lunched at a select, sequestered hotel, whose entrenched guests talked golf and food. When a middle-aged man came into the dining-room, aggressively maiden ladies pounced on him with their laughter. This must have been one of those funk-holes for the privileged said to be numerous in the Lake District.

"Conversation seemed consciously localized, the golf course their Eastern Front and in what direction lay so-and-so a matter for controversy. In a cage by the door a parrot was perched in silence. Every woman as she came in bent first over the cage with a cheerful greeting for Polly: this was their ritual, as much so as in other places where wirelesses were now being switched on for the News. Immobile during their quips and cluckings, the parrot stared at them through the meal with cold, hostile eyes. And suddenly, at the height of their chatter and brittle meaningless laughter, he squawked, a hideous, grating squawk."

For two weeks at the end of June I got away from it all, to quintessential England, that enchanted region I had discovered on two pre-war walking tours with Duncan, Shakespeare's other-Eden, demi-paradise.

Stratford-upon-Avon, gateway to the Cotswolds, was full of RAF men, all the hotels commandeered, stripped of luxury, echoing to boots on bare boards, the clatter of tin mugs at wooden tables. I shared an attic room in a ramshackle riverside house with a Canadian soldier, who was diligently snapping his way around the starred sights of England on leaves from Aldershot.

"It seems funny to me," he said, looking down from the window at the sun-drenched Avon, "when you call these streams rivers. In Canada . . . " He had been to see *A Midsummer Night's Dream* and couldn't see anything in it.

I went to see *A Midsummer Night's Dream* and came out to walk beside the river "at the magic hour when light on grass and trees is golden and shadows haunted". But the poetry evaporated; it was 1942; a girl was perched, laughing, on a bicycle crossbar in front of an RAF officer; they followed me into the churchyard and became silent, kissing under a tree by the river. They are nearer the Athenian wood than I, there is fire in their veins, while I, following darkness like a dream, am cold with fantasies. Late that night the bombers started throbbing over, headed in close formation for the North Sea and Germany.

From a carriage window next day the Canadian, who was called Rick and had been a waiter in a Toronto hotel, looked out at the orchards and half-timbered farms of the Vale of Evesham and talked of limitless prairies and the Kicking Horse Pass. We had tea at the White Hart in Moreton-in-Marsh and he noted carefully in his notebook that Charles I had slept here. I saw him off at the station and set off, rucksack on back, north-east for Chipping Campden.

Up in the evening hills, the hedgerows pungent with honeysuckle and wild rose, I leaned on a gate to count the spires. An old man on a reaping machine clattered out of sight over the brow of a hill. Three village boys ran waist-deep through corn to a pool hidden in a copse. I could hear splashings and shrill cries and glimpse the naked limbs of boys and girls. I reached Chipping Campden in time for dinner at the Noel Arms. It was like coming home.

After dinner I climbed through wheat and mustard fields and nettle-grown copses to Dover's Hill and lay on the ridge that thrusts out like a prow over the valley. The huge sun was a smoky red behind the haze of far hills. On the steep slope below cows moved nearer, tearing at the grass with wet mouths, breathing and coughing like old men. In a hollow an airman lay with his girl, closely embracing.

I walked four hot days in the Cotswolds, through Upper and Lower, Great and Little villages, whose churches provided cool retreats from the sun and the spinning road. I would throw off my rucksack, sit in a pew or against a cold pillar, and read the epitaphs of boys and girls, of beneficent squires and fecund ladies, of philanthropic spinsters who proudly 'died in a virgin state', of youth cut off in its bloom.

26

" . . . In Youth nor Beauty there's no Trust," ends the epitaph for Mary Crips, who died in 1739 aged 19 years, "For I had Both and yet am Dust". Near the village of Great Rissington, which cannot have materially changed in two hundred years, a girl in Land Army breeches, young and graceful, comes swinging down a wheatfield path, her brown arm balancing a scythe, the sun in her eyes.

Of Burford I wrote to Michael, a former schoolfriend, now an Army lieutenant awaiting embarkation: "Standing on Burford bridge towards dusk, the time of late swallows and bats, you can look into the Windrush and its dark or luminous reflections and feel that such a moment, this silence now, would be in exile a stabbing memory. I, who have lost nothing and can still after two years of war eat trout and strawberries at the Bull and lean on Burford bridge, have no right to vicarious melancholy. But if I had to fight it would be for such moments and such places."

In London I rowed Molly on the Thames at Richmond, took her to the Café Royal and *The Man Who Came to Dinner*, spent a day and night at her Hayward's Heath home, where her parents and younger sister were charmingly discreet, got my arm round her in the back stalls of the local cinema during *Dr Jekyll and Mr Hyde*, unsatisfactorily kissed her, and left still brooding on my virgin state. By November, when I came to London as a reporter on the *News Chronicle*, she had joined the Wrens and was writing spasmodically about depth charge classes and invitations to uninhibited ships' dances.

CHAPTER FOUR

Letter to my mother: 13 November, 1942.

"When last night I rang the bell of a house of which only Victorian pillars and a freshly painted door were visible in the misty dusk and a lady in a sweeping gown appeared, I wondered if I had not missed my way and stumbled on a society dinner-party. No, it was Mrs Monckton, showing me up with precise cultured greeting. Her age is indeterminate, perhaps a well-preserved 35.

"And then my room . . . I rubbed my eyes. Siegfried Sassoon's peacock-blue flat in Gray's Inn was not so far removed – except that my colour-scheme is cream and apple-green. Subdued luxury – tall reading-lamp, gas-fire (with meter), tray drawers, cupboards, h. and c. washbasin, all concealed: two cushioned easy chairs, divan bed, two upright chairs, a polished oval table with flower-pot in bowl, evergreens in a bowl on the mantelpiece. My room overlooks the trees and garden of this Pimlico square and fifty yards away soars the spire of a church. I hear its mellow chime now."

Letter to my mother: 22 November.

"I apologize for so long a lapse. The real reason for the delay is the bewildering atmosphere of my first week in London: a bewilderment that has left me during leisure hours slightly 'out of key', with a wandering fancy that is not conducive to letter-writing. It is therefore difficult to say what my work and colleagues are 'like'. I could answer 'easy and pleasant' but that is too summary to be wholly truthful. It is all very different from Manchester, which was by comparison parochial. Busy, efficient, almost abrupt, this is at first a difficult place in which to establish intimacies, which is naturally disconcerting.

"My colleagues – all, of course, a good deal older than I – are quick, intelligent, cultured. Books I have seen being read during periods of inactivity – which are prolonged – include Plato, *The Bible in Spain, Pride and Prejudice*. To the left of my desk sits an American who is shortly going to North Africa: to the right a woman who before the war was the Rome correspondent.

"Today I have been to the Tower on the off-chance of seeing General von Thoma pacing the battlements. From Tower Bridge, the grim and massive walls and towers and turrets, faintly lit by a blood-red sun, looked more steeped in history than anything I have yet seen.

"It is a great pleasure to see from my window after breakfast the winter trees hazy in mist and bonfire smoke. I have discovered so far three characters regularly on view: the milkman calling his lagging horse: a gardener sweeping dead leaves for the bonfire: and a young man in a fur coat who strides round the square in an imperious way, tugging behind him a commonplace dog.'

They were lonely, those first weeks in London. In the Bouverie Street office off Fleet Street, an over-awareness of my comparative youth and inexperience made small talk an effort and suggested stand-offishness. I felt that acceptance had been achieved when Ian Mackay, the Industrial Correspondent, a benevolent giant of a man, with a mane of unruly hair and the bluntness of a Highland Scot, lumbered one evening across to my desk, said "New boy? Come and have a drink," and down in the Mucky Duck (alias White Swan) yanked out a new top set of false teeth, clapped them on the bar and hollowly boomed, "That's better – now we can talk."

We were joined by Richard Winnington, the film critic, like me a compulsive pipe-smoker, who called almost everybody 'Cock', had an incisive tongue and sharp wit, and whose company I came to seek for arguments disconnected with newspapers. "You don't know what you're talking about, cock . . . " and we were away.

Just to be part of London, with a room of my own, gave a sense of achievement. Some of my most awesome childhood memories centred on a holiday at my paternal grandmother's in Palmer's Green: of being jolted inside a horse-cab while yellow fog swirled around a coldly-flaring lamp post: of riding on the open top deck of a tram with spiral stairs along a street of shops that went on for ever: of climbing skywards at the Zoo to be lifted on to a box on an elephant's back: of a moment of terror at Madame Tussaud's as the bosom of the corpse-like Sleeping Beauty suddenly, jerkily, drew breath.

The London I sought now lay buried in a remoter past. With Christmas in the air I explored the narrow alleys, the courtyards and dark, chill churches of the City, lunching at the George and Vulture and Simpson's, but failing to raise the comfortable ghosts of Pickwick and the Cheeryble Brothers amid the too, too solid businessmen talking shop and war and smut.

I spent Christmas Day at the office, the wireless exuding synthetic cheer, kicking a paper ball about with the assistant news editor and a couple of messenger boys. At night Mrs Monckton threw a party for her lodgers. We ate roast goose, squashed round tables in one of the bed-sitting rooms, pulled crackers and put on paper hats. There was Mr Sadkowsky, a gaunt elderly Russian, two Free French officers, a Major Thomas, a Westminster Hospital medical student (who had a skull called Elsie hanging over his bed), the secretary of Admiral of the Fleet Sir Dudley Pound, Mrs Monckton, her twelve-year-old daughter Anne and 'Granny'.

It was not until eighteen months later that I was to be put wise about Mrs Monckton. Small, dark, volatile, I could imagine Hilda Leighton finding her a very gracious lady indeed. She must have been attractive when she was younger, I thought, but now there were wrinkles under the make-up and a faint air of desperation about her vivacity. Coming back from the office after an early turn, she would invite me into her cosy ground-floor room for a drink and a chat. She spoke in a rapid, soft, cultivated voice, smiling often. Her husband was in the army and she seemed devoted to him. Her mother, who had an Irish accent, did most of the heavy chores around the house and could sometimes be heard rowing violently with her daughter, whose voice on such occasions sounded a good deal less cultivated.

During the Christmas dinner we all, with varying degrees of conviction, kept up a semblance of festive merriment, if only for the sake of Anne. She really did seem to be excited and enjoying herself when she shepherded us up to her room, where a Christmas tree glittered, with presents for all. Afterwards, at her request, we played blind-man's-buff for nearly an hour, with intervals for refreshments. When he was caught Mr Sadkowsky groped around with very little enthusiasm at all. One of the Free Frenchmen seemed quite eager for his turn, when he would make for where Mrs Monckton had been before the blindfolding. She laughed protestingly when he caught her and did not immediately identify her. I did not record Major Thompson's contribution to the game, but noted that Granny could have put on a more cheerful front, if only for the sake of Anne.

From the Philistine ramparts of the provinces, one of the main lures of London for me had been the imagined coteries of poets, painters and composers, talking the night away in a fine frenzy as once their ancestry had done in the Left Bank cafés of Paris. I felt I appreciated that line of Ezra Pound, "I am homesick after my own kind", although aware that, if ever I got into such coteries, I had precious little to show in the way of creative output.

During my third month in London I met for the first time my painter cousin Rodrigo. I knew little about him in a family context except that his father, my father's elder brother, had gone to South America and become something of a black sheep, and that his mother was Spanish. Rodrigo was always referred to as 'Bertie', perhaps because it had been his father's name and had a comfortably ordinary ring about it.

Rodrigo had already made a name as a painter of still lives and portraits. There was a current exhibition at the Leicester Galleries which the *Sunday Times* had designated "From Matisse to Moynihan". He sounded eminently worth being homesick about, and when I met him at Aunt Maria's flat in Marylebone I was not disappointed. He looked quite unlike any other relation, more Spanish than London-Irish, with a rich, masculine voice and the assured, slightly cynical air of a man of the world.

His mother looked very Spanish, which of course she was, speaking with a charming, broken accent, and his wife Elinor, one of whose haunting paintings of aetherial schoolgirls wandering by a misty river hung on the wall, was charm itself. Over supper they referred without a hint of pretension to numbers of 'names' they knew in degrees of intimacy, but awe was dispelled by the relish with which Rodrigo talked of Philistine relations we shared.

Rodrigo was in the Army, lecturing up and down the country on camouflage (later in the year he was appointed a War Artist), but during his leaves I spent a number of evenings at his Maida Vale home. The house was Victorian, a 'period house of character', and faced a tree-lined canal with humped bridges. Inside it was agreeably cluttered and lived-in. We sat in a room looking out on the overgrown back garden with trees that at twilight diffused a bottle-green glow. They were evenings of rambling talk and laughter, doubtless run-of-the-mill for Rodrigo and Elinor, but for me tinged with a magic I would never find in Fleet Street bars.

Of the first visit I wrote: "There were two other women present, Barbara who lives there and a strange creature, Daphne, who looked languidly from under a wing of pale hair and said curious things like 'What's the need for affection? Why can't everyone be on their own?' and 'It's rather awful when you come to realize that you hate your father and mother'.

"We drank a lot of tea, talked about a lot of things from *Paradise Lost* to large families, and played Bach and Mozart on an out-of-tune spinet. A desultory query about pollen and bees launched a fantastic conversation fostered by an encyclopaedia. Not least of our discoveries was that one of the occupants of an ants' nest is the blind and colourless wood-louse, *Platyarthrus Hoffmannseggi*. Like a club bore, Rodrigo suggested, only tolerated because of some defect. But, reading further, we discovered that he was being uncharitable. The blind and colourless wood-louse has thick tufts of hair which the ants suck."

I later learned that Daphne, who had a way of coming out with unconsciously outrageous or strange remarks at which, to her vague surprise, everyone fell about laughing, was Stanley Spencer's girl. She is to be seen, riper-looking and less willowy than I remember her, in a number of his massive groups and her portrait is in the Tate. I saw her later that year in the Piccadilly Kardomah having coffee with Stanley Spencer, who looked tiny, wizened and dried-up beside her. He was nagging her in a high-pitched whine and she looked vaguely unhappy like a vulnerable young governess being bullied by a precocious and petulant child. I did not dream of intruding and when I passed the table Daphne showed no sign of recognition. By then Rodrigo had faded somewhat from my scene. His was an older, maturer generation to which I did not rightly belong.

My father, whom I met on his Board Meeting trips to his London head office, was not a fluent letter-writer. It was the letters from my mother that brought with them the enveloping warmth of home. To all of us, wherever scattered, she wrote with the same outgoing of loving concern and interest. One could plainly see her at her desk in the drawing-room, eyes focused through her reading-glasses at a pen that seemed to glide of its own volition from line to line, mouth slightly open in concentration.

She had had a cosy fireside tea and long chat with Doris Fardon: Rupert Greggains had been awarded the MBE and his mother had posted fifty letters recording the fact: Geoff's last term at school began tomorrow and she felt sad already, but not Daddy who wasn't soaked in sentiment like her: Mil only just didn't have her left hand fingers sliced off in a farm machine: so very nice I had met Cath and visited John Bunyan's birthplace: how bad that I had to work on Sundays – it was so easy to fall into apathy.

The fact that apathy, towards Calvinism at least, had long since overtaken me must have been apparent to my parents, though it in no way deterred their exhortations and veiled reproofs. Even for their sakes I could not bring myself to attend a Lord's Day service at the Strict and Particular Baptist Chapel in Gower Street or a garden fete at the Aged Pilgrims' Friends Society at Hornsey Rise. The gulf between my inherited faith and my evolving self was widening. After a night of Soho pub-crawling, to pay a duty visit to Aunt Alice at Pine Cottage, West Worthing, was like stepping backwards into the pages of *The Way of All Flesh*.

Aunt Alice was a retired headmistress of whom even my mother and her other sisters were in some awe. I could remember her in childhood casting a chill on Christmas games of skill because of her unswerving determination to win them, even at the cost of childish tears. She had a direct gaze, a dominant voice and shrill laugh, pince-nez and hair drawn tightly back from her temples. One could imagine her as a well-meaning dragon brooking no slacking or insubordination around her classrooms.

She had greatly mellowed in retirement and, during my two-night stay, was charming, attentive and interested. Her grasp of world affairs was only distorted by her bracketing together of Hitler, Stalin and the Pope as anti-Christs. 'Popish' to her was an epithet no less sinister than 'Nazi' or 'Communist', and she saw the hand of Rome, that Scarlet Woman, in the most unlikely places. She had even detected it at work in the editorial offices of *The Times*, which had been her favourite paper but which she had ceased to subscribe to because of the prominence given to utterances from the Vatican. She had switched to *The Telegraph*: the *News Chronicle* was much too radical for her taste.

The only person Aunt Alice was known to have been in awe of was Mr Popham, the Strict and Particular Baptist minister at Brighton, that same Mr Popham from whose selected sermons Mr Shaw the postman had so interminably read. During a childhood holiday at Pine Cottage, she had taken me and Rachel to tea at his home and had seemed to hang on his every word as though he had been a latter-day Prophet of the Most High. To us he seemed pompous, affected and as tedious as his sermons.

In Pine Cottage, a delightful house, choicely furnished and immaculately kept, life was ordered with the regularity of a school time-table and the piety of a comfortably-off elderly spinster who had walked unscathed through Vanity Fair but was in no great hurry for the Promised Land. There was a tear-off Thought for the Day in the lavatory. After breakfast, prompt at 8, which was prepared by Winnie the Help, a lame, scowling woman who constituted something of a cross to be borne, Aunt Alice opened the Bible by the teapot and read the Old Testament portion for the day. By the fireside after supper the Bible was passed to me and I was asked to read the New Testament portion. It was something I had not done since boyhood family prayers at home, and I felt as Samuel Butler's lapsed hero must have felt had he been trapped by Christina on a duty visit to the Rectory.

"Thank you," said Aunt Alice when I had done. "Shall we pray?" She knelt beside her easy chair and I did likewise on the opposite side of the hearthrug, instinctively closing my eyes, then opening them again to look at the Dutch tiles. Aunt Alice prayed in the general terms approved by the Elect: she prayed for victory 'if it be Thy will', she prayed for Winston Churchill, whom she venerated in a different but no less intense way than Mr Popham, calling him 'Winnie' but regarding him as a kind of cigar-smoking Mr Valiant-for-Truth, and then she prayed for me. Not at great length, but enough to make me stare harder at the Dutch tiles.

I felt it would sound a bit complacent to say 'Thank you' when we got up. After a suitable silence I asked if the Dutch tiles were from Delft. I was wondering how she would have prayed if she had known how I had spent the night before last.

Letter to Duncan, February, 1943:

"I met John Atkins, literary editor of the *Tribune* at the Café Royal. After some beers a couple of pseudo-Bohemians, both under twenty, joined us. The elder, who came in with £3 worth of new books under both arms – Donne, Dante, Coleridge and some obscure Chinese philosopher – had been pestering Atkins with stories and articles and had to be told delicately that they were unsuitable.

"He handed me his most recent story to read, an esoteric and adolescent trifle with a Baudelaire poem as its climax. I told him I didn't like it, but had perhaps missed the point as my French was hazy: whereupon he translated the poem – cold kisses and arms like snakes – in a loud resonant voice: stumped for one phrase, he called across two tables for assistance. Oxford to the core, intolerant, vain, he was not without a charm of boundless exuberance.

"His younger friend Mark, seventeen and Cambridge-bound, was small, plump, good-natured and wore a huge velvet tie.

After Atkins left for home about 9.30 he offered to be my guide into La Vie Bohème. The three of us walked, loudly arguing about something, to the 'Swiss', a pub packed from bar to walls with young and older men, some extravagant hangers-on, some genuine artists (Dylan Thomas, for example, who is either drunk or unhappy), many of them abnormal, Lesbians etc., here and there a soldier marooned and disgusted in the swarm.

"I suppose I was disgusted but realized it afterwards and while I was there drank and enjoyed myself. You just say anything, no one cares much, get caught up with a pale glamorous actress, return to the attentive Mark for introductions to more 'quite good' poets and artists. Some of the young men were just appalling and complete fakes, others I would like to meet sober.

"Around closing time Mark suggested the night would not be complete without a visit to a nearby club. A hefty Board of Trade girl we were with went in search of 'Elizabeth' to make a foursome, but found her on an Indian's knee, so the three of us set out through the dark alleys off the Tottenham Court Road. Around what looked like a warehouse door a crowd of noisy men and women were struggling to get in. The club was full to the doors and from some of the creatures who pressed for entrance I was not altogether sorry, although I felt ready for anything. An RAF man recognized the hefty girl and they made off down an alley. After a while I said goodbye to Mark and John Sylvester who had arrived with a bevy of friends and walked unsteadily to Trafalgar Square and a bus."

As Fate would have it, this unplanned foray into La Vie Bohème proved a curtain-raiser to a long-running study of the nocturnal goings-on in the pubs of Soho and Chelsea, made possible by my office. A totally unexpected assignment meant that, for a considerable period to come, I would have four days and nights off every week, to do with as I pleased.

CHAPTER FIVE

The Ministry of Information was housed in London University's skyscraper building in Bloomsbury, and it was there I led a claustrophobic, troglodyte existence three days and nights a week for fourteen months from March, 1943.

The British and foreign correspondents whose job it was to keep their ears glued to the Governmental horse's mouth ("It was officially announced last night . . . "), to wade through a blizzard of communiqués and handouts, to chat around for useful background and to dash to their telephone booths when the occasional hot news was announced, occupied a large windowless ground-floor room that had been used for student lectures. The *News Chronicle* desk and two phone boxes were in a corner by one of the entrances and there I was set, unbeknown to me at the time, to win my spurs under the initial tutelage of Syd Fearn.

Syd was a sports writer, a slow, gentle, unflappable, grey-haired, tweedy character without whose soothing presence I might on occasions have found myself screaming "Let me out!" as the sixteen-hour stint crawled past midnight under the in-exorable glare of the strip lighting. He treated me with a kind of avuncular benevolence and reminded me of a Home Counties Bill Leighton, though not given to drinking bouts. He talked about soccer epics he had witnessed, about his wife, about his garden and about the novels of Joan Grant.

This last seemed strangely out of character. I could picture him clearly in his orderly suburban semi-detached, hob-knobbing with a neighbour over the garden fence, the epitome of the solid, blinkered Englishman who was proving the despair of Hitler and Goebbels. But under the spell of Joan Grant, whose mystic novel of Ancient Egypt, *Winged Pharoah*, had become a recent best-seller, Syd had begun to swim gently out into unfathomable waters.

In the same deep, measured tones with which he delated on his marrows or his wife's arthritis, he spoke of Horus and Ptah and Anubis and Seth and the terrors of the Underworld. The idea of reincarnation fascinated him. Looking at his lean, handsome profile as he talked, fiddling with the pencil on his desk, spectacles slipped down his nose, I tried to place him in a tomb-painting. Probably he had come way back in the procession among the priests, more purposeful-looking in short-skirted tunic than tweeds.

Our desk was on a ledge that ran round the room, with steps down into a kind of arena. The desks (actually tables) were spaced evenly throughout the room and in the late hours when there was nothing doing and the silence of ennui had settled, our rival correspondents sat in drooping isolation, islands entire unto themselves.

There was the unlikely *Express* man, who sported yellow waistcoats and herring-bone suits, a suave, sprightly character one could imagine focusing field-glasses at a point-to-point: the heavy John Bullish *Telegraph* man who fussed and blustered: the elderly *Mail* man who wrote erudite detective novels, talked with the commanding tones of a don and kept his files in immaculate order: the *Herald* man, who looked belligerently at the world through rimless glasses, an iconoclast and a rebel, whom I found particularly congenial: the *Times* man, tall, with a gentle smile, who commuted by motor-cycle, and on rainy days divested himself of waterproof cape and leggings as though sloughing a secret skin to reveal his professional self: the *Mirror* man, a lone wolf, who became abusive in his cups, exposing a fascist streak, and who fastened on me for company to Syd's growing disapproval ("He's no good. Watch him, Mike, watch him.")

Of the foreign correspondents I was particularly intrigued by the Norwegian and his wife, who kept themselves to themselves, painstakingly swopping notes for their rival papers: the Finn, a withdrawn man with the expressionless moon-face of an Eskimo, who gave the impression of living in a private world of his own: and the Chicago correspondent, rugged, brusque, unsmiling, whom one could imagine in a Hemingway story and on whose table would perch one of the prettiest girls around the Ministry. She was pretty in a cool, fragile way and I could not believe she was the nymphomaniac she was made out to be.

There were quite a number of pretty girls in the different divisions of the Ministry, and, so I heard, quite a lot of sleeping around. The only girl I took out was Cynthia, who worked in the photographic division and daily changed the war pictures in the showcase in the corridor outside our room. She was a friend of the nymphomaniac's, more openly flirtatious, perhaps because she was not quite so pretty and anyway married. I was not surprised when she told me she had considered nursing as a career. One could see her, brisk and attractive in her starched uniform, placing a cool, firm hand on a fevered brow before passing on to the next bed with a smiling "You'll live!"

I took her out to lunch occasionally, where, apart from Ministry gossip, she talked about her family, the millinery department of John Lewis's where she had worked and the husband she had recently married, now in the Middle East. One night off I took her to see a play about the wives of fighter pilots. Over supper afterwards she chatted as though we hadn't been to see a play at all. But in the taxi outside her flat she didn't ask me up and I was relieved to see her at the showcase the following Monday smiling in the same mock-challenging way.

There was a feeling of unreality about these months at the Ministry, of being less at the hub of things as out of the swim. It was an enclosed world, wheels within wheels, and the academic associations of the vast building were reinforced by the numbers of arty- or intellectual-looking men and blue-stocking women one passed in marble corridors or rubbed shoulders with in the spacious high-up canteen and poky bar. I would watch with envy a relaxed, animated group centring on Cecil Day Lewis, looking every inch the poet, before getting back to an office demand for the total tonnage of merchant shipping sunk during the past six weeks.

I had read with fascination the M.O.I. episodes in Evelyn Waugh's *Put Out More Flags*, and kept my eyes open for prototypes of Ambrose Silk, the aesthete queer who, as representative of Atheism in the Religious Department, would send copies of a Swiss report of Storm Troopers attending a requiem mass in Salzburg to 'Free Thought' and 'Godless Sunday at Home': of Geoffrey Bentley the publisher, who had introduced a pair of marble busts by Nollekens into the former chemical laboratory where he was getting out "a very nice little series on What We Are Fighting For: I've signed up a retired admiral, a Church of England curate, an unemployed docker, a Negro solicitor from the Gold Coast, and a nose and throat specialist from Harley Street".

It was only in retrospect that I fully appreciated the bizarre character of our own daily round. There was the morning lecture at which a Brigadier would tap and drone over a map of the battle-front in such a schoolmasterly fashion that one could have replaced the imagined gunfire barrage with the whistle of Agincourt arrows or rattle of Waterloo musketry: or where shorthand would suddenly start to flow as a Chindit back from Burma revealed that cobra steaks taste rather like chicken. There were consultations with the uniformed and civilian Advisers of the three Services, of whom the least likely but most forthcoming was the distinguished theatre and music critic Philip Hope-Wallace, as much an authority then on the marshalling yards at Dusseldorf as on Molière or Mozart. There were the hagglings with the censor over the deletion of seemingly innocuous copy. There was the telephone tussle after an air raid with the *News Chronicle*'s blustering, neurotic night news editor, who refused to accept that we could not find out exactly where bombs had dropped and who, we knew, was chiefly concerned to know if any had dropped at Beckenham, where he lived with a spinster sister who made his private life a misery.

As the clock ticked towards ten o'clock on Wednesday morning, we would be waiting impatiently for relief to arrive in the person of H. de Winton Wigley, a burly, bucolic old-stager with a Chaucerian eye for the girls, and his assistant, a thin bespectacled shorthand-typist. The three mostly deskbound days and nights and the few hours of fitful sleep on a three-tiered bunk in the stuffy basement had left us mentally and physically dehydrated. To emerge through the portico of this monstrous hive of relative inactivity into sunlight or wind or even rain was like a prison release. Ahead stretched four whole days of freedom, the world (the limiting factors of war and a nine guineas a week wage aside) my oyster.

A tinge of guilt would sometimes obtrude as, back in my snug bed-sitter, I settled in an armchair facing the plane trees of the Square garden, to open an envelope firmly inscribed 'On Active Service'. The least I could do was to keep a morale-boosting correspondence going, a kind of there'll-always-be-an-England reassurance. Weather permitting, I would spend a day, sometimes two, country-walking, shaking up the liver, clawing away the mental cobwebs, seeking contact with the 'real' England. Buckinghamshire with its footpaths through beechwoods and farms to open hills, its still-isolated villages, its river-paths, became a substitute Cotswolds.

'The Thames near Marlow' was the heading to a letter to Duncan I wrote on a day when Rommel was launching an offensive against the Eighth Army in Tunisia, the Americans were sinking 10 Japanese warships and 12 transports off New Guinea, the Russians were withdrawing across the Donetz in the face of 25 German divisions and Berlin was about to receive its heaviest raid of the war.

"At High Wycombe, after a good lunch at the Red Lion, I stood in the High Street heavy and drowsy and without energy to walk those few miles to Marlow. A country bus took me, two long rows of people facing each other, heavy brown wives going home to put the kettle on and wonder if they'd lay jam for a treat, a shy RAF man with a nastily possessive WAAF in spectacles, a slip of a schoolgirl suppressing a smile of pride as she paid her fare. Glances slipped away, would not be met, the bus panted up the long steep hill leaving High Wycombe a warm roof-jumble. The rising fields behind the hedges were summer-serene: a man and a cart poised on a crest, sky at his back.

"I walked through Marlow without lingering, to the Thames, the blue brimming water where swans idle away the hours under the church, under the green-hazed trees, where the elderly fishermen mess about with bait in tins and never seem to catch fish, and where this afternoon a succession of Spitfires thundered tree-high, metallic brutes, startling everyone but the swans – one after another, rolling to show their powerful bellies. The throb of engines troubles the sky all day, but walking alongside the river, with the sun in your face, you are almost back in the pre-war peace of rivers – boats on the Dee, the Cam, the Isis, the Avon – birdsong everywhere. I wonder shall we ever find those days again on the lovelier Thames?"

My constant companion in numerous pub-crawls around Soho and Chelsea that, with occasional theatres and concerts, interspersed the country walks and the Ministry treadmill, was Ben, an Irish architect whom I had got to know slightly when he was a wild, authority-defying student in Liverpool, where his habit of wearing a rope round his neck marked him off from more conventional students. We found that we laughed at the same kind of things – Beachcomber, Miles N'Gopaleen of the *Irish Times*, Restoration Comedy ("Body of me, thou'lt answer for that, muckworm . . . "), James Joyce (though here he was far more attuned to the nuances of dialogue and incident), culture-vultures, Americans, Old School Tie types ("I say, old boy, steady on.") In the relaxed intimacy that is to be found in the anonymity of pubs, we assumed the roles of outsiders, rebels without a cause, lone wolves.

We probed very little into each other's backgrounds. Ben had six brothers and three sisters, some of whom he met on visits to Dublin but who appeared to play little part in his life. His father was dead. The only person of whom he spoke with real tenderness was his mother. He was a lapsed Catholic, as I a lapsed Calvinist. His creative urge was as meaningful but undisciplined as mine. Whether his sex life was as unsatisfactorily sublimated I could only guess. We did not talk about such things and got on the better for it.

In London Ben was working on Professor Patrick Abercrombie's Greater London Plan. He found nothing bizarre in the slow evolution of this massive blue-print for a finer, more civilized Capital while the bombs, and later the rockets, were still nibbling away at it and the war was by no means won. The drawing-office at the Ministry of Town and Country Planning was for him as the news room at the Ministry of Information was for me, just another part of the forest we couldn't see for the trees.

Soho and Chelsea were the nightly stamping-grounds for a variety of writers and artists, few of whose names would have meant anything to the general public, and a larger number with no pretensions to creative talent who were either hangers-on, alcoholics or sex-obsessed. One rarely heard the war mentioned except in terms of its nuisance value and it was difficult to imagine how most of them spent the daytime hours. The idea of there being any remotely parallel sound of drunken revelry by night in Berlin or Tokyo was inconceivable.

In the early stages of an evening Ben and I would limber up over pints of bitter watching the play develop in our chosen pub. We had soon sorted out the leading members of the cast, known or unknown, by their dress, voices, mannerisms, capacity for drink. Some moved restlessly around in groups and were to be found in pubs in both districts. Some kept to the same pitch in the same pub, only to be shifted if the beer ran out and there was a concerted move to a pub down the road. On some occasions the beer shortage was widespread and one would follow groups in the blackout waiting for the grapevine to spread the word – 'Cross Keys', 'Black Horse', 'The Highlander'. An air raid, as later the throbbing drone of a doodlebug, had little or no effect. Ben had never been inside a shelter – "a waste of good drinking-time".

Apart from Dylan Thomas, who had a way of focusing attention wherever he went, the dominant character was Tambimuttu, always known as Tambi, an Indian born in Ceylon, who edited *Poetry, London* and usually had in tow a weird entourage of sycophants. Soho, or more exactly a concentration of pubs just inside Bloomsbury, bounded by Oxford Street and the Tottenham Court Road, was his nightly beat. He was often accompanied by another Indian called Subra, who wrote short stories and was by comparison stolid and down-to-earth.

Tambi was willowy, with *café-à-la-crème* skin, flashing eyes, a charming toothy smile, a mop of fine, blue-black hair which he smoothed poetically back with the long curved fingers of a hand. When he talked, in a rapid lilting voice, he made great play with his hands, dangling them in front of him and flicking the fingers at you as though they were made of rubber. He flicked his tongue, too, like a chameleon, between his white teeth, pink against the purplish lips.

Although he not infrequently got drunk, I never saw him buy a drink, even for himself. He had a reputation for being unscrupulous about other people's money, as about their girls. At first we thought him effeminate but this was not so. Aspiring poetesses who came into his orbit, like moths to a flame, were more likely to be appraised for their bedworthiness than their talent. It was doubtless Tambi on whose knee 'Elizabeth' had been sitting that night at the Swiss.

Poetry, London was a lavishly produced magazine which contained some good poetry and a lot of pretentious nonsense. Tambi didn't much like talking about poetry. Once when I mentioned W.B. Yeats he said in an off-hand way that he had never read him. "I don't need to," he said, flicking his fingers. "I know what is good poetry. I know instinctively. I have flair."

There can never have been a period when the itch to write has been so prevalent. I have met a number of my generation who, like me, wrote verse or kept diaries with little thought of publication, more as a personal reassurance that they existed and that life was not as meaningless and cheap as war could sometimes suggest. The impulse might have been the same in the coteries of Fitzrovia, but the motives were different. Getting into print was the goal. *Poetry, London* apart, there was a generous outlet for new talent – *New Writing, Modern Reading, Selected Writing, English Story, Horizon, Lilliput*, not to mention the 'little magazines', like *Seven* and *Phoenix*, that flared and fizzled out. They must all have dealt liberally in rejection slips.

It was in the vague hope of finding a Not Impossible Poetess that I answered an advertisement in the *New Statesman* inviting communication with a Box Number with a view to "exchanging views and constructive criticism". I received a reply from a girl called Shirley who said that she was a music student who was keeping a War Diary and had written two psychological novels as well as a lot of poetry. Her brother, now in the RAF, was also extremely interested in poetry and, *she* thought, wrote very well himself.

The two poems she enclosed were rather off-putting but I suggested meeting for tea followed by *Heartbreak House*. She was not exactly plain, but rather hard-looking, purposeful and aggressively matey. I could see her in a white dress in the front row of the contraltos singing her head off in The Messiah. She wrote next day saying she had enjoyed *Heartbreak House* and hoped I had too, ("One thing is quite certain – that Shaw enjoyed writing it!") and went on to a needlessly elaborate criticism of a sketch I had sent. She promised to send me a story called 'Seduction, 2nd Class', and enclosed two more poems. One was called 'Out of Town':

> Carpet my floor of dreams, o secret night,
> Ending all knowledge of tomorrow.
> And let the dark rear up its friendliness
> With soft and shielding flexures,
> Then will I lie in dim perception
> Of rain against glass
> And the rattling of wind-troubled door handles.
> Happiness is white cloud
> Lightly dispersed by the ack-ack
> Of dying men, sacrifice,
> The inutterable weary longing of solitude.
> And while we wait in passionless dread,
> The bastard seed of murder weapons
> Is spurted into the uterus of our very being,
> With blood of the ravishment child.
> In such an era
> Only the imaginations of night are real.
> And you who share my thin ledge of uncertainty
> Will know this, too.

I wondered, in my reply, whether Tambimuttu might like it for *Poetry, London*, though not going so far as to suggest that he might care to share Shirley's thin ledge of uncertainty.

CHAPTER SIX

One evening Ben told me about Carola. She had started work in the Town and Country Planning drawing-office, was a niece of Lady Tweedsmuir, John Buchan's widow, was a talented painter and wrote poetry, was beautiful, intelligent and he knew I would like her. I had half-guessed something was in the wind. There had lately been a constraint to his laughter, abstracted pauses, even an unprecedented disinclination for what he called 'great store of flagons'. I felt a twinge of aggrievement but said I would love to meet her.

We met in a pub called the Woodstock, a long way from Chelsea and Soho, and I found that Carola *was* beautiful, intelligent, kind, understanding, gay, discerning. We met from time to time as a trio for a theatre or pub session and occasionally Ben would revisit with me the Chelsea haunts, but with none of the old devil-may-care abandon.

I sought other company, including a Frenchwoman called Rita whom I had met through an old schoolfriend, Michael's elder brother Peter, an up-and-coming architect. She had a picturesquely Bohemian studio flat with steps going up to a kind of platform, which was her curtained-off bedroom. Ships' figureheads in a leafy patio and a pet terrapin testified to her absent sailor husband.

Rita was a patroness of the Arts, about which she showed more enthusiasm than knowledge, and loved having a circle of artistic people around her talking of the Arts. She would listen approvingly, occasionally interjecting a comment of her own that showed her enthusiasm and lack of knowledge. She was small and dark, her face yellowish and rather moist-looking, and she had a pronounced foreign accent which she used to embarrassing effect when she was in one of her winsomely flirtatious moods. She struck me as a kind of culture-conscious Hilda Leighton, impressed but kittenish among her clever Boys.

Ben's happiest recollection of her was after a National Gallery lunchtime recital by Franz Osborn, piano, and Max Rostal, violin, whom Rita was assiduously cultivating. She had button-holed them in one of the Galleries and was enthusing when Ben came up. "I do so love that quick passage in the Beethoven. You know—" Max Rostal eyed her balefully. "To which quick passage do you refer?" he asked in his richly guttural accent. "Please be more specific. Beethoven is *rich* in quick passages."

After another recital Rita invited me to lunch with them. "How did I play?" Rostal asked Osborn. "I don't know," said Osborn. "I didn't hear you. I was listening to myself." "That is what it sounded like," said Rostal. Rita trilled delightedly and glanced at me in a way to suggest that wasn't it a privilege to be hearing two such artistes letting their hair down. She shot me a profounder glance when Osborn let fall that he was dining that night with Edith Sitwell. "She wears these rings?" she asked in a knowledgeable way. "Enormous rings," said Osborn. "And she takes snuff." Rita almost purred.

A highlight of this period, recorded at length in the diary-turned-journal, and in a letter to my mother, was a visit to the writer I then most admired, laureate of childhood, seer of the supernatural, Walter de la Mare. I had written to him during my dog-food days at Morrell's, the only fan letter I ever wrote except one to Nova Pilbeam, whom I had fallen in love with in an Alfred Hitchcock film. She did not reply but de la Mare did, at some length, to my astonishment and delight.

The romantic-sounding address on a more recent letter from him, The Old Park, Penn, Bucks, suggested a goal for one of my country jaunts, this time a country bus from High Wycombe climbing through beech woods to deposit me on the village green at Penn, high in the Chilterns.

The journal's entry indicates that, as this was to be a private not a professional visit, I had made no appointment to see de la Mare, and that for some time, in a shiver of anticipation, I walked up and down outside the high, holly-topped wall around

47

The Old Park before entering through a narrow gate marked 'Private'.

"The drive swerved uncertainly through wooded parkland. Two cottages in the foreground and a mere glimpse of a green roof in trees made approach tentative, and shrill rooks overhead advised retreat. I enquired, nevertheless, at the first cottage and was directed to the green roof. Beneath it a substantial white house materialized. I knocked at the door.

"It was opened by a tall, unpoetic-looking man wearing riding breeches and a high-necked jumper. I delivered my prepared introduction which he summed up with somewhat disconcerting brusqueness, as though he had heard it before: 'You've corresponded. He's with friends, but I'll tell him.'

"I was left by the open door facing a long, low-ceilinged hall, in which two elderly ladies leaned across a table in earnest conversation. Behind them French windows commanded a blue distance of wooded hills. Escape now being out of the question, I felt more at ease. And when de la Mare appeared it was with reassuring friendliness that he welcomed me in and led me upstairs to his private study.

"It was a spacious yet cosy room, firelit, with Chinese prints on the walls, bookcases brimming over, a desk littered with corrected proofs. He settled in an armchair opposite me, lit a cigarette and began asking questions.

"He was much as I expected he might be: baggy tweed suit: small but with a noble head: aquiline nose, features strong but gentle: calm melodious voice: if anything like a benevolent hawk, with eyes that were attentive but focused beyond.

"But most of the next forty minutes were far removed from the kind of talk I had imagined. He questioned me on the technical side of journalism, on the legal aspects of interviewing, and showed special interest in a murder case currently in the news. Trying to draw him away from such mundane matters, I asked him about Penn, particularly its ancient church and churchyard in which I had carefully browsed, and was amazed when he spoke disparagingly of 'worn-out tombstones' – this from the author of *Ding Dong Bell*, the prowler in darkness, the connoisseur of dust and ashes!

"In the hall he offered to show me down to the bus stop by the green. A wind had blown up and rooks' nests tossed black against a reddening sky. It was the setting for a de la Mare story, haunted and haunting. That wind-buffeted walk in the gathering dusk must surely have inspired a less earth-bound conversation, but, thinking of those waiting friends, I declined. 'I hope we may meet again,' he said, and stood for a while to watch me go.'

Writing later to invite me to tea at his flat in Twickenham, he apologized for his "rather inhospitable welcome – there was a sort of reunion of friends at the time". It was only then that it occurred to me to wonder what other grand old man of letters would have excused himself from a circle of intimates to closet himself with a stranger. Was it curiosity as much as courtesy? The never-answered de la Mare question-marks: Who? Whence? Whither? Is there anybody there?

When the meeting did transpire two months later, it was in circumstances that made me wonder whether I should have been there. A number of notes and telegrams making arrangements and cancelling them had gone before. On the train to Twickenham the picture I had in mind was of a cosy huddle over a tea-trolley with just de la Mare and the 'old parson friend' he had mentioned. Then, at the Twickenham ticket-barrier, I saw in front of me John Atkins, the literary editor of the *Tribune* I had met at the Café Royal. "D'you live here?" he asked. "No," I said. "Actually I'm going to tea with Walter de la Mare." He stiffened. "So am I," he said.

I had an awful feeling that there had been a mistake about dates when we were ushered into de la Mare's flat in an elegant Queen Anne house at the end of Montpelier Row to find two other guests already seated at the fireside. One was the poet Rostrevor Hamilton, the other an old doctor friend. I had by then discovered that Atkins was professionally interested in de la Mare and had met him before.

Like everything else in the flat, the china and silverware of the tea-table reflected our host's exquisite taste. But the table-talk was of a rarer refinement. It was talk such as I had never heard before. Afterwards I recalled less of its content than of the imperceptible way in which de la Mare lifted the conversation into another dimension, where the barriers between dream and reality dissolved, and one almost questioned that we were sitting round a table eating bread and butter and blackcurrant jam and having tea poured for us from a silver pot.

A part of my mind was absorbed, carried away, a part distracted by a nagging feeling that I had not been expected. Only once did de la Mare draw me directly into the conversation. He was much given to ending a fantastic, hypnotic monologue with a question. Somehow the talk had got round to the war in Russia and of the latest news of a battle raging around a hill near Stalingrad. "A hill," said de la Mare, musingly, turning on me his dark, far-focused gaze. "What do you think of? A hill . . . "

I said the first thing that came into my head. " 'There is a green hill far away/ Without a city wall . . . ' " De la Mare pondered the image for a moment and then smiled. "Yes," he said, "a green hill."

De la Mare's reply to my letter of thanks showed my discomfort to have been groundless ("Gate-crashing indeed! I shall look forward to another talk either here or at Twickenham again – how good *that* talk was."), but the war took over and I did not meet him again. It was not until a year after his death in 1956, aged 83, that the publication of a book called *Tea with Walter de la Mare* put my brief encounter into perspective.

It was written by one of de la Mare's many guests, Sir Russell Brain, a Harley Street neurologist, who had early decided that "his talk was so good, and so unlike any other conversation that I have ever listened to, that when I got home I wrote down what I could remember of it". Guests as diverse as Lord Wavell and Joyce Grenfell, Lady Asquith and Siegfried Sassoon, I discovered, had fielded questions odder than my 'hill'. ("Do you dream in colour", "How much of your past life would you not find boring if you had to live it again"). More privileged than I had imagined, it had been for me an oasis to look back on when war closed round and life became cheap.

There were evenings when I sat alone in my bed-sitter, listening to the sounds of life in other rooms – a pacing of footsteps, a brisk cough, a humming or whistling – crediting my fellow-lodgers with far more incisive and purposeful activities than my desultory scribblings. In coming across Hazlitt's essay "On Going a Journey", I had at least found a reassuring justification for my unaccompanied jaunts into the country.

"I like solitude, when I give myself up to it, for the sake of solitude. Give me the clear blue sky over my head, and the green turf beneath my feet, a winding road before me, and a three hours' march to dinner – and then to thinking!"

In my case the thinking would sometimes involve the weaving of words into verse, partly an exercise in technique, partly to encapsulate a thought or mood. The results were hardly of the kind that Tambi would have jumped at, nor would the fact that earlier specimens had met with the approval of Walter de la Mare have been likely to impress him. They seem sad now as faded snapshots.

I stayed one night in a Wendover hotel, talking by the fireside with the pretty wife of an airman who lay wounded in a nearby hospital, and later in the bar with two seedy strolling minstrels, attached to ENSA, one a dejected middle-aged comedian, the other a 16-year-old boy from Hull who played the accordion. All through the night army convoys rumbled with grinding gears through the narrow streets. Next morning I climbed the steep high hill behind the village to find gunners occupying the summit and encamped in the woods around.

That day I walked ten miles or so along a beautiful wooded valley, thinking of that hill as it might have been, and of myself as enigma.

> Look where he lies, that foolish man,
> Prone on the hillside in the afternoon.
> His pipe is cold in his clenched fist,
> His strange desires all sleep at last.
>
> We in the valley knew him well,
> A restless man and we took it ill
> When he left the village before daybreak
> That he told us nothing when he came back.

Back with mud on his boots and his hair
Blown by the wind and a look in his eyes – of fear?
Silent he sat in our company but some
Declared his eyes burned bright as any flame.

His friends were few and secretive
But ready at any time to scoff
At rumours of women, a private grief, they said
He climbed the hills and walked in solitude.

He has it now and quiet he lies
On the green slope where the wind blows
Over the hill, across the sunlit plain,
He is cold in the sun: he lies in the wind like stone.

Letter from Diana. Bath. February, 1944.
"The Admiralty deadens me. It's unthinkable to take any genuine pride in work which will gain you no advancement because of your youth, which is my fate. N.B. I am *not* a Wren you maniac. I am a Temporary Civil Servant which is practically the Seal of Doom (not Basil). *That's* why the M.O.I. goings-on interested me because I wondered how they compared with Admiralty machinations.

"It is difficult to explain without sounding like something out of Ethel Mannin, but always I have an intangible but distinct feeling of frustration, that the sands of life are running out without my living it. The reason why I tell you is because I seemed to detect a similar sort of unspoken, unformed, perhaps unacknowledged dissatisfaction in you.

"Of course all the facts point to my being quite wrong: I mean you have a good and absorbing job, doing what you want to do. You almost certainly have a circle of interesting and amusing friends – and yet. If I could speak French I should express myself better – there seemed an air about you that you were only half-alive, and I'm *not* being rude, because some of the time it disappeared – for example at the Trocadero. Yet when dinner was over and everyone fell out into the blackout, you

52

shut up again like a clam – I could almost hear the snap – and said something like 'Well I must go back to work. See you sometime,' and I felt maddened and suddenly unenthusiastic, and that the wall which you seem to put up was quite unclimbable."

Diana was a Birkenhead friend of Mildred, with whom I had wept many a tear of laughter at crazy party games at home, but now, seeing her on her own or with friends, could no longer regard as 'one of the family'. She was on the large side but shapely, with dark curly hair, lively brown eyes, a slight drawl to her resonant voice and an infectious laugh. Her letters, in a bold, flowing hand which I was to welcome in many a still-undreamed-of posting from Normandy to Japan, were warm, colourful and often very funny. I had vaguely equated her with John Betjeman's "Pam, I adore you, you great big bounteous sportsgirl", although she wasn't that big and, though she did play tennis, was far more at home in a smart Bath cocktail bar, Kempinski's off Regent Street or the Bull at Burford.

The letter, written in a rare, or rarely-admitted, 'melancholy and introspective mood', rather threw me and I hastily ransacked my ivory tower for a suitable reply. Whatever this turned out to be, we did not again trouble the 'hidden depths' and looked forward to meetings in London and Bath.

Bath, to which much of the Admiralty had been evacuated at the outset of the war, was the most elegant of stamping grounds for the Senior Service. In its lively bars, though partnered by non-Wren Diana, I sometimes felt conspicuous in civvies, and tried to picture myself as one of them, a naval type.

In Bath I renewed the acquaintance of Gilly, who had treated us to the Trocadero dinner. He was a good deal older than either of us, a charming, gentle man who held a hush-hush job in the Admiralty and was, I guessed, more than half in love with Diana. What on occasions I noted about him, and mentioned in a letter to Diana, was a subdued, almost stricken air about him. Her explanation was as shocking as anything I heard in the war and, switching my thoughts back to the start of the war, made my pacifist soul-searchings seem trumpery.

"You are right, Gilly's life has been tragic: and yet he remains unembittered, even when his favourite son who was a boy with

Quaker friends and ideals died as a result of treatment in a political prison near Glasgow. Gilly had a lot of letters from him written in this prison, which showed the gradual mental deterioration that overcame him – so much worse than the physical ill-treatment he received.

"These men were deliberately broken in spirit which often resulted in the breakdown of their health. Gilly toyed with the idea of showing the letters to Winston with a 'Here's your free England for you', but he didn't because he said he realized in time that humility is the important thing in life. I was amazed and horrified that such barbarity exists in this country, and awed by Gilly's humbleness of mind.

"It was perhaps a mercy that the son died soon after his release, because I think Gilly's heart would have broken to have had to watch the result of a sensitive and delicate mind being coarsened. When he was released he spent each day in bars and pubs, waiting for it to pass. He didn't care whether he lived or died, and joined a sort of suicide squad which went about making bombs and mines harmless. Gilly said they were all quite mad. They used to try and kill each other by ghastly practical jokes such as seeing who would walk slowest away from the bombs before they went off. Can you wonder that the steadfast sweetness of Gilly's nature amazes and awes me?"

Letter from Martin. Lahore, India, May, 1944.

"Congratulations on the news that you are earmarked as an invasion correspondent (if there is an invasion!). It is a grand assignment. I wonder how you got past the doctors, or don't you have a say? Do you get any special training as a war correspondent? I should think it would be necessary."

A summons from the Editor had jerked me from the somnolence of the Ministry. From behind his desk Gerald Barry, cherubic but keen-eyed, had asked me about life at the Ministry, about my health, listening with an occasional nod of his head. "I think you'd better get a uniform," he said at last. "See Ronnie Walker. You'll be working under him."

Walker, an Australian although you wouldn't have guessed it from a rapid, impatient voice that ended on a squeak when he was excited or annoyed, informed me that he was to cover the wider, strategical aspects of the air war from SHAEF head-quarters, while I accompanied the Second Tactical Air Force into the field. Once they were firmly based in whatever part of France we were going to invade he would be taking over from me. What I did then was not his business. I would need to get a medical check-up for possible operational flights.

When my turn came at the Air Ministry building in Kingsway, the doctor sounded me, tested my blood pressure, then handed me a tube of mercury. "Blow," he said. I blew and the mercury crept nearly half way up the tube, quivered and sagged. "Come on, right up and keep it up. Don't mess around. There are others waiting." I blew hard but with little better effect. The doctor frowned and consulted the form I had filled in. "Ah . . . Grade Three . . . War Correspondent . . . Oh well, that'll be all right."

In due course a tiny photograph of me appeared on the Leader Page at the tail-end of nine others, under the headline "These Men Cover The Second Front".

"MICHAEL MOYNIHAN. Collaborating with Walker, Moynihan comes new to active war reporting from a long probation as specialist in winnowing news from much Ministry of Information chaff. He is the youngest of the *News Chronicle* team and will cover the tactical side of the air war."

Letter from Aunt Jane. Bristol, 5 May.

"We are now taking the *News Chronicle*, for your sake, so saw your pretty picture with the nine others, and shall look forward to your effusions. Not so much for war news as *your* account of it.

"Well you know our hearts – we pour them out every day at the throne of the heavenly grace that you may be *preserved* in every sense of the word and in due time return to your own vine and fig tree.

"Aunt Grace says if you are shipwrecked on our coast – just call here and you shall have of the best our estate affords.

"Much love ever, J.A.

" 'I will lift up mine eyes . . . ' "

CHAPTER SEVEN

SCENE: An orchard, Somewhere in England.
TIME: D-Day minus 27.

From my camp bed I look through the open flap of the
tent at apple trees bathed in early morning sunshine, a distant
cow, and, in the foreground, Courtenay Edwards of the *Daily
Mail*, in trousers and vest, washing his shaved face from a
brand-new, collapsible canvas basin. After a final sluice he
whisks his towel from a guy-rope and begins to sing, in a
loud, cheerful, unmusical voice:

> Maresie dotes and doesy dotes
> And littlelambsitivey.
> Kidderleativey too.
> Wouldn't you?

Everything about Courtenay is brisk and assured and efficient. He looks perfectly at home in the blue battledress in
which I feel dressed-up as though for a charade. Shaving from
a mirror dangling from a tent-pole and washing in a canvas
basin in a Sussex orchard might be the most natural thing
in the world. His field-kit, bags, portable typewriter, binoculars, despatch-case, are neatly arrayed as though for inspection
around his bed. They make my lot look a dump.

The orchard encampment near Chichester is a temporary halt
before we new correspondents are distributed around 2nd TAF
bases. We have been paired off under Conducting Officers, all
of them Battle of Britain fighter-pilots, whose job it will be
to drive us around, put us in the picture, arrange facilities
and generally keep an eye on us.

Our Conducting Officer, now stirring on his camp-bed at the back of the tent, is Flt Lt Gerald Fisher, tall, lean, handsome in a rakish way, with blue eyes that screw up when he gives a rather twitchy smile, which he frequently does. He was shot down in his Spitfire but has assured me that he had a screw loose before that anyway. This was in the Farmers' Club in Chichester yesterday afternoon, where Fish had no trouble at all in gaining an entrée ("A couple of war correspondents – I'm showing them around"), and where we drank beer, of which there is a local shortage, and played darts with the natives.

Now the other tents are stirring to life, and from the field kitchen wafts a smell of frying bacon. Birds are singing. Courtenay wipes his spectacles with a crisp, folded handkerchief and takes a deep breath of orchard air. He ducks into the tent, smiling under his moustache, rubbing his hands. "Come along there, now," he chides. "Arise and shine."

The weeks before D-Day, that cataclysmic event awaited so long that one had begun to wonder if it would ever take place, were spent moving from airfield to airfield, getting to know Group Captains and Wing Commanders, drinking in dank tents or carpeted messes with the pilots whose bombs were now raining down on the airfields and ground installations of Northern France. RAF stations like Thorney Island in Hampshire had an orderly, regulated, almost collegiate air about them – meals round long tables, dormitories, notice-boards, a spacious officers' mess with armchairs, silver cups and trophies, attentive stewards. Coming out of echoing corridors into sunlight on a vast expanse of green, one half-expected to hear the click of cricket balls instead of the scream of fighter-bombers taking off.

Courtenay, later to become motoring correspondent of the *Daily Telegraph*, was far more technically clued up than I and would rattle away on his typewriter in an unnerving way, though very little of what we wrote got in. It took me some time to distinguish between the silhouettes of Spitfire, Hurricane and Typhoon, despite the patient expositions of Fish. He was almost as enthusiastic and knowledgeable about fighter aircraft as about racehorses, boozers and birds.

Eighteen days before D-Day we took part in a raid by Mitchell medium bombers on a target 30 miles north of Paris. I had never flown before and from the co-pilot's seat of R for Roger peered down fascinated as the hedged fields, copses, farms and roads around Dunsfold grew toy-like as we climbed. We flew high, England a patchwork quilt far below, the Channel a glittering stretch of ribbed water, then France another patchwork quilt far below. I sat bunched in parachute and Mae West, in a kind of limbo, the drone and throb of the engines muted by the earphones, an occasional cackle of voices on the intercom soon ceasing altogether. Above, below and on either side of us the three squadrons of Mitchells flying in box formation, rising and dipping in the sunlight, gave a cosy, protected feeling.

I made mental notes as the countryside unrolled – deserted roads and railways, rivers unrippled by craft, clusters of bomb-craters like half-rubbed ink stains on a green and brown carpet, two puffs of smoke suddenly blossoming ahead of us and drifting by. We seemed to have altered course but still the countryside stretched almost barren of human life, occasionally a truck or motor-car like ants on a ribbon. And then ahead a glitter of ribbed water. I felt a nudge. Flying Officer Desmond Martin from New Zealand was looking at me quizzically over his mask. He pointed to a dangling cord. I was switched off.

I replaced the plug and the cackling sounds enclosed me. "Did you see them go?" came his sudden voice. For all I knew he had been making observations for my benefit for quite a while. I nodded. "Bang on," he said. "No flak to talk about."

Fish was waiting in the mess with a celebratory drink. Courtenay joined us, rubbing his hands. "Nice, quiet trip, eh! See any flak?"

It was a Saturday evening and we had plenty of time to file. But what? Nothing had happened. All I had seen was a patchwork quilt. Then it occurred to me that this was the story. I wrote about the deserted roads and railways and rivers of Northern France, of a daytime 'dead land' where the enemy lay so low you would not guess he was there. It came out on Page One on Monday as 'Desert Scene – Hitler's Front Line in West', datelined Advanced Base, Sunday, and with my first by-line.

I received a congratulatory telegram from the Foreign Editor and a message was passed on from Ronnie Walker that the 'flags were out' in Bouverie Street. I had some more celebratory drinks with Fish, who found it all very amusing.

"It is D-Day. Our ships have sailed. At nine o'clock tomorrow news of the invasion will have been announced. We must give our troops all the support we possibly can. God knows they will need it." It was an 'Advanced Base' Station Commander talking to correspondents in his tent at 10 p.m. on Monday, 5 June, in front of him a map arrayed with pins and crayon lines in red and blue. I heard all this the following day. Fish and I were in London at the time.

We came back on the train to Havant kicking ourselves with chagrin at having accepted assurances that nothing was in the wind. I was galled not to have sat in on that historic, long-awaited announcement, though it was of no real consequence. I filed as dramatic a story as I could of rocket-firing Typhoons in cat-and-mouse encounters with armoured vehicles and staff cars on roads leading to the Normandy battle area, of tired-eyed pilots sitting in circles on the grass impatient for the next trip. I did not expect it to be used. For a four-page paper covering D-Day it was very small beer.

Small beer would have been our portion for the six weeks after D-Day, during which we chafed at the bit in our no-longer Advanced Bases, had it not been for the flying bombs, or Pilotless Planes as they were initially known. The first four dropped on 13 June (in Sussex, at Gravesend, Sevenoaks and Bethnal Green) killing four and injuring nine. By 16 June 73 out of 144 that crossed the English coast reached London. On 18 June one dived on the Royal Military Chapel at Wellington Barracks during morning service, killing 131 and seriously injuring 68 members of the congregation. General Eisenhower ruled that for the time being flying bomb targets should take precedence over "everything except the urgent requisites of battle".

My first flight to one of the lairs of Goebbels' 'Hellhounds' proved abortive when piled cloud turned us back with bombs unreleased. Before lunch next day Fish and I were having a drink in the Thorney Island mess when word came that Mitchells were going out for P-plane targets at 2 p.m. We made the 40 miles to Dunsfold in a 30 cwt truck at breakneck speed to arrive at the airfield at 2 p.m. precisely. The Mitchells were lining up for the take-off. We rushed for the hut where equipment was kept. "Too late," said the officer in charge, but Fish was already grabbing at parachute, Mae West and helmet. "Get into them," he said and made a sprint for the nearest Mitchell. When I got there he had attracted the attention of the pilot and was shouting up, "Can you take a passenger? Here he comes." The ladder came down and I scrambled aboard.

As we taxied to the runway I leaned back to the navigator. "Where are we going?" He produced his map and stubbed a finger on a small green strip, a nameless *bois* somewhere in the Pas de Calais area. Over the Channel the Australian pilot told me over the intercom, "We're in the first box. There's plenty of flak and we may have a rough trip."

This time I remained plugged in, heard the navigator's "Target over the port wing", peered down at a narrow wood about half a mile long, heard "Bomb doors open" and "Here we go" and from the two Mitchells behind us, watched two neat clusters of eight 500-pounders drop in a seemingly leisurely fashion to their goal.

The flak came, but for the second box. I saw the six Mitchells circling beneath a cluster of black puffs. "Miles too high," reported our gunner. "They haven't a clue . . . Now they're getting the range. One poor —'s flying on his own. They're after him all right." The lone Mitchell was surrounded by smudges but got through.

Back at Thorney Island I learned that Ernest Hemingway had been flying in the second box, though not in the straggler. He regaled the young pilots in their mess that night, in a man-to-man way, with anecdotes from his past, but fell somewhat in their estimation when they later read his highly dramatic account of what to them had been a routine assignment.

My account appeared under the curdling heading "I Went Bombing a P-Plane Wood", which Martin, writing some time later from India, said had set him singing "Polly-Wolly-Doodle All The Day". Five days later when I flew over burning

Cherbourg in a Mosquito, the subs let me off more lightly with "From a Mosquito, he saw the doomed city on fire". They omitted a mention of some of our ships firing on us on the way back across the Channel. It had been an 'unofficial' trip laid on for my benefit by a Wing-Commander who said he wouldn't mind having a dekko at Cherbourg himself and could fit it in nicely before lunch. The Mosquito was a plane that even I could non-technically recognize as a thing of beauty. Squashed into the tiny cockpit beside the Wing-Commander it was like riding a Derby winner after the plodding Mitchells.

Letter to my father. 19 July, 1944. Normandy. "I cannot say where we are based except that with some twenty other correspondents I eat in a tent and live in a château. The aged Duc and his wife have a few rooms to themselves and potter about the garden and extensive grounds, rather lost among the airmen, soldiers, tents, jeeps. Last Sunday morning I was roused from a deep sleep [we had arrived in the early hours] by hymn-singing. From my bedroom window I looked down on a Service around the lily pond. It was broadcast. General Montgomery read the Lesson, the Parable of the Good Samaritan, in his clipped, headmaster's voice. The Padre's sermon was poor – the wonderful élan, the laughter and comradeship of the Troops ad nauseam. Other correspondents are billeted at a Norman castle nearby where William the Conqueror is said to have planned D-Day 1066.

"I feel well bedded down now – the exhilaration of seeing the French coast at night lit by chandelier flares, red tracer bullets, gun flashes, of driving in darkness through the first villages, has worn off. So too has the confused feelings of the first day or two. We work in groups of two with a Con-ducting Officer. Normandy is open to us as far as we care to venture and we make our own programme. We have seen most of the places that were or are in the news – Bayeux, its ancient streets packed with soldiers, long queues for food or drink at the Lion d'Or: Caen, its suburbs terribly dev-astated, its hospital crowded, the remaining citizens living in squalid shelters. We went to one in a cellar: children, aged women, dogs, huddled on mattresses in the gloom. On our first visit the Germans were still within 600 yards of the city centre.

"But war is very different from my imagination of it. There is no 'front', only a field that might be hiding snipers, villages still unbroken. Guns are thumping all day, nearer you hear machine-gun fire. I was chiefly impressed at first by the traffic. Roads are congested everywhere, with endless convoys throwing up clouds of acrid, choking dust. The countryside reminds me somewhat of the Cotswolds – the same mellow stone, orchards, wheatfields. The peasants carry on as they can, their villages mutilated, cornfields scarred by tanks. But they wave and smile and a publican will take you into a back room for a glass of calvados or wine.

"You will have seen my story of the bombardment east of Caen. It was unforgettable. My only discomfort were mosquitoes that plagued us all night as we tried to sleep on the grass waiting for it to begin. I am still a mass of irritation. Yesterday we called back at the POW camp I mentioned and found it chock full. At close quarters the German seems an insignificant creature: there were a few arrogant or bestial faces, but most looked half-witted or very scared.

"All the time one must resist a feeling of entire pity. War is more than anything a terribly squalid business. On the wireless or in a paper it appears clear-cut, a question of strategy, gains and losses. Here you see files of hang-dog prisoners, churches, farmhouses, cottages, mined and passed over, where tanks have come to grips and men died by the hundred. You see a field lined with fresh graves, wooden crosses with only a name and regiment, and behind a screen dead men bound in blankets, awaiting the padre. You see a jeep travelling very slowly over a rutted path with two wounded men on stretchers, one clenching his fist, a hospital plane packed with stretcher cases. Near the front you steer clear of a house or wrecked tank around which clings the loathsome sweet smell of death.

"That is one side. The contrast is here too. The corn is being reaped, a milkmaid crosses a field with pail and stool, a watercarrier leads his oxen, boys fish in a stream. At this moment from the village across the fields comes the clang of the church bell. That is the life, thank God, that will go on. I must come back here one day to walk country roads on which only a trap or haywain passes, drink wine in the café of a quiet village where sounds are country sounds and the scars of war have healed. It is for that contrast that I would not for anything have missed this experience. War cannot be read about, it must be seen. Because death over here is a commonplace, lasting things increase in significance. The mind reaches back for a firmer faith.'

We were billeted at Creully, a nondescript little village apart from the castle and château, a stark 18th century edifice behind ornamental gardens running to seed. The wing where the Duc and his wife lived had a notice by the door, 'Strictly Out of Bounds'. When it was left open you glimpsed a cool tiled hall, with a fox's head on the wall and a staircase spiralling out of sight. I felt sorry for the Duc, who rode horseback around his estate, gazing austerely ahead as though we were all wraiths inhabiting another dimension. His wife, wearing a floppy straw hat, went snipping among her rose-bushes with a basket on her arm and the same air of remote preoccupation. It was not until after the war that I learned that in one of the rooms up that spiral staircase they were harbouring two German officers.

Whoever had occupied the four-poster in which I slept had bequeathed me his fleas. I bathed in the deep clear pool over the meadows which was much frequented after hot dusty days on the roads, resembling a nudist colony. But fleas accompanied me to the camp bed in one of the tents behind the château to which I was moved with my new sparring-partner.

Courtenay, who was not one for pubs though in no way a prig, had not approved of Fish's conducted tours of Sussex and Hampshire in search of pubs that had not run dry and regarded him as a bit 'wild'. He had teamed up with an elderly, conscientious *Telegraph* man, and I had been joined by a man who, for reasons later apparent, I will call T. He was a brisk, stocky character, a great talker, who could effortlessly hold the rapt attention of a bar as he related an episode from his eventful and dramatic past or told the latest Shaggy Dog Story.

T. had been in the army at Dunkirk, about which he was reticent to the extent of suggesting that he could not bear to think back on the ordeal. He had shrugged off the idea of making operational flights from England as a 'waste of time'. "You fly over a P-Plane wood – so what?" He was a Jekyll and Hyde man, in his cups becoming loud and abusive, a moist look spreading over the pallid skin of his face. Over calvados in one of the few bistros open in Caen he had suggested spinning a coin with Fish as to who should take the pale girl who served us up to bed. Fish had declined. Although equally a man of the world and equally a fluent talker, he told me he thought T. 'a bit of a bounder'.

The Caen bombardment was preceded by a briefing by Monty in a huge marquee to a mass of correspondents, including a *News Chronicle* colleague, Larry Solon, who was attached to the British 2nd Army, a dry, witty, incisive American, whom I had dined with at the small hotel in Creully where he had taken a room to get away from the regimentation and incessant shop-talk of the castle. Monty put us in the picture, with the aid of maps and diagrams, in the clipped didactic tones of a lecturing headmaster and the young staff officers in attendance on him could be seen as favoured senior prefects, all-rounders, jolly good chaps. There was no whiff of death or destruction in the air.

We took up our positions on a hillside overlooking Caen just before midnight, with six hours to wait for our grandstand view of the Greatest Show on Earth, with a cast of thousands, an epic certain to rate rave reviews from the assembled critics. The mosquitoes began to whine and bite . . .

I scratched myself in the morning sunlight sitting at a table outside the château where I had brought my typewriter away from the confident clatter in the camp. This was my first Big Chance. The clichés bounced about in my head like peas in a pod. The Duc appeared through the door marked 'Strictly Out of Bounds', paused fractionally as he passed my table, then walked on. I began typing.

"OVERLOOKING THE CAEN FRONT, TUESDAY.

"At dawn today there was total eclipse over the Caen front. The rising sun vanished behind a vast canopy of black smoke billowing from the greatest concentration of bombs ever loosed from the air.

"From this eminence a mile and a half west of the Orne I saw a spectacle before which the mind reeled and language became dumb. The final fury of warfare that, in a space of minutes, could turn the first flush of dawn into impenetrable night.

"We took up our position on the road near Benville, overlooking the German line, before midnight. 'Operation Clobber' – the greatest air offensive ever directed against an enemy battlefront – was due to begin at 5.45 a.m.

"Throughout the starlit night the skyline was illuminated by gun-flashes, shell-bursts, the occasional cascading gold of flares. Within a few hours, we knew, there would be no more firing from across the Orne.

"In airfields throughout England the crews of nearly 6,000 Allied aircraft – heavy bombers, medium bombers, fighter-bombers – were preparing to deliver the most shattering blow ever inflicted in the history of warfare. The plan had been worked out to the last detail. Every man in the huge armada soon to take to the air knew his job.

"First the heavies of Bomber Command were to obliterate the two sectors where German resistance was strongest – the steel factory of Mondeville which faced us now across the river, and four villages to the west, Touffeville, Sannerville, Banneville and Emieville, where the enemy's strongest gun emplacements were situated. For each of these two targets 450 Lancasters and Halifaxes were detailed.

"Their mission accomplished, Marauders would stun enemy resistance in the centre of the area – the villages of Cuberville, Demouville, Goberville and Cagny – employing fragmentation bombs to avoid cratering the ground across which our tanks and troops were soon to advance.

"The U.S. Air Force had the next role – 300 to attack Troarn, 700 to attack Bourgebus, Tilly-Campagne and Bras.

"Around the area of devastation rocket-firing Typhoons would be on the prowl for 'targets of opportunity' – guns, tanks, anything that attempted to escape the holocaust. On a wider arc long-range fighters of the U.S. Ninth Air Force would carry out similar reconnaissance.

"This was the plan for 'Operation Clobber'.

"Along the hilltop, as the grey light glimmered into orange behind the ruins of Benville, we waited and wondered.

"A lark rose from the cornfields in front of us to pour down song from the brightening sky. Down in the valley a cock crowed. In the gathering light we could plainly see now the outline of the factory across the river – the factory which was 'going to be removed'.

"The hour struck. It was 5.45 – zero hour. A Mosquito, marker for the greatest force of destruction in history, was over the factory.

"There was no question as to the accuracy of those bombs. From the bulky humped mass of the factory two pink clouds were sprouting, spreading in smoke.

"In a matter of minutes everything was in confusion. From behind us, to the north and south, an artillery barrage broke into a cacophony of noise. Above, thunder was rolling across the sky.

"We held our breath at sight of the approaching air fleet – heavy bombers pouring from behind the horizon until the sky seemed to shudder.

"Across the river as the first bombers went in gouts of black smoke poured from the factory. Another Mosquito came in to shower the golden rain of its marker with deadly accuracy.

"Now the ground under our feet was shaking, and from the western skyline night was creeping up the sky. The smoke rose, impenetrable, blue-black against the ripening corn before us, until it was no longer possible to see bomb-burst or marker.

"Soon even the incoming bombers were veiled behind the drifting clouds. The pale summer dawn, quiet but for the whine of shells and a lark's song, had been terribly transformed.

"It was night now, a night of smoke and thunder, thick with the fumes of gunpowder. Only one streak of light penetrated the unnatural murk – a bomber shot down like a fiery arrow. Later I saw a Flying Fortress fall in flames, one member of the crew floating above. Out of the whole force I saw no other casualties.

"There was nothing to see now. The landscape was blotted out and the fog of destruction was creeping to the road where we stood.

"We made south – to find the sun risen, a blood-red above the woods. But here too as we watched the smoke followed – and the vivid flashes of 25-pounders shot through a gloom.

"We made in a roundabout way for Caen. In every village we passed men, women and children stood at their doorways and in the street, silent, watching.

"I called at a prisoner-of-war camp and was taken into a pen where two Germans lay huddled beneath blankets. One was 19, one 32. Both had the eyes of the hunter turned hunted. I asked them what they thought of the bombardment. "We are better off here," said one. And the other, "Since Christmas I have known that all was up."

"We entered Caen. Smoke hung over the city. A formation of Fortresses, silver in the sunlight, faded into the murk and shutters down the scarred street vibrated to new thunder.

"In Caen, some 400 yards from the river this incredible morning, we found a bar open and washed the taste of dust from our mouths with white wine.

"As we drank a figure appeared at the end of the street, coming from the river. It was a man, and as he came near we saw the sweat bright on his unshaven face, his clothes dusty and ragged.

"He had come from south of the river – a Christian from the City of Destruction.

"We brought him into the bar and gave him wine. He talked wildly: "I was sleeping. This came. I put the mattress over my head. I escaped."

"He had forgotten everything, it seemed, in the terrible inferno, except that it was morning and he must go to work.

"And he left the bar and went down the street to mend roads."

That afternoon we went back to the POW camp. It now had an additional 1,655 men and 40 officers. In a pen by himself sat a Brigade Commander, tight-lipped, immobile. According to Polish deserters from his brigade he had issued orders that no British soldiers were to be taken alive. Armed or unarmed, wounded or helpless, all were to be shot. "A man like that deserves to be shot out of hand," said the camp commandant, who was taking us round. "But he will be tried according to law."

Next day we drove to Caen, to the factory which 450 Lancasters and Halifaxes had 'removed'. A number of tough-looking Canadian soldiers were roaming about among the ruins. German survivors of the holocaust were being winkled out from holes and cellars.

There were dust-shrouded kitchen gardens, hens and tame rabbits running loose. We heard a squawking and saw a Canadian holding a flapping hen by its legs. He pinioned the wings and cut off the head with his knife. He put the decapitated body down and watched it run, stagger and collapse.

A corporal in shirt-sleeves approached us from behind a crumbled wall. He was a small, wiry man, his weasel-face grimed and unshaven, his eyes glazed. He had a revolver and two Lugers stuck in his belt. "Want to see some fun?" he said. He took us behind the wall, where seven Germans crouched, their faces blank, empty of feeling.

Fish, shaken despite all he had said about the Hun, looked at the corporal and said he couldn't mean it. The corporal looked from Fish to T. and I, flicking his eyes over our British War Correspondent shoulder-flashes. His lip curled. "Why don't you get back where you belong? This is a war. I've had mates killed. Why don't you bugger off?"

There seemed to be no officer around. We said we would report him. "Do that, bud," said the corporal. "Do that."

Back at Creully we reported the incident but I never heard if anything came of it or whether those seven Germans made the POW cage. As Fish said, 'resisting capture' or 'attempting to escape' were pretty watertight alibis.

CHAPTER EIGHT

The road to Cherbourg stretched straight and switchback to
the horizon and Fish kept his foot down on the accelerator.
We were getting away for the weekend from the dust-choked
roads of the British sector, the stuffy tents, the monotonous
grub, the longeurs of camp life.

The war had settled down to a slogging match south of
Caen and the 2nd TAF were lying low. From an Auster two-
seater observation plane the front was seen as a dead-looking
countryside of brown seared fields, pock-marked with craters,
of woods and orchards stripped to black charred trunks, of
villages dust-coated ruins.

Norman Cliff, the Foreign Editor, had cabled me after
the bombardment despatch: "Congratulations your magnificent
story Caen stop Colleagues proud of you stop", which suggested
an unlikely edition-time scene in the Feathers or Mucky Duck:
"I say, have you read Mike's piece?" "I certainly have. Don't
know about you, but I feel proud of him." But only three
of twelve stories I had sent in the first three weeks had
got in. I had taken the opportunity of a letter from the
Editor to suggest that I was probably easily the lowest-paid,
if youngest, war correspondent, and had been given a 'bonus
as war correspondent' rise to 12 guineas a week, presumably
reviewable after the war. I felt there was sufficient justification
for a sojourn in the American sector.

We spent the first night in an untouched fishing village in
Brittany, scrambling around rock-pools, basking in the sun,
eating fresh lobster and drinking wine. Now, on the road to
Cherbourg, T. suggested that a drink was indicated and neither
Fish nor I disagreed. We stopped at a shabby wayside café under
trees which, like others we had passed, had a notice outside:

'Out of Bounds to Troops'. Fish explained to the proprietor that we were actually civilians in uniform, British at that, and we were served rough cider at a table in a dark little room. It was a potent brew. We had more. Raised voices and laughter must have carried. An American Military Policeman darkened the doorway. 'Can't you read?'

The justification for ignoring the sign which had satisfied the proprietor did not impress him, particularly as it had been far less amicably put. He looked sourly at us and told us to get going. T. looked him up and down with that Hyde glint in his eyes and the slightly moist look to his skin. "Why don't you run away, sonny boy," he said in much the same tone the Canadian corporal had used to us. "Go on, sonny boy. Push off." The M.P. looked daggers and left.

We finished the drinks and came out into the sunlight. The M.P. was talking to another M.P. in a jeep across the road. Fish and I walked casually to our car. T. made for the trees. The two M.P.s came over and asked for our passes. We showed them, with some bluster about reporting the incident ourselves. They took down particulars and drove off. The fact that they had not troubled about T. suggested that it had been a mere formality, a cautionary exercise of authority. T. came out from the trees where he said he had been having a leak. "What did you want to give your names for?" he said. "Bloody cheek." We got in the car and Fish put his foot down.

Cherbourg was unrecognizable from the smoking city I had looked down on from the Mosquito six weeks ago. Ruined buildings drab with dust looked as though they had always been that way; G.I.s lolled and chewed and looked bored. We had lunch in an army canteen where Fish chatted up a likely-looking Yank about the brothel situation. "No dice," said the G.I. "Out of bounds." But Fish got an address. "They're civvies in disguise," he said, twitching at T. and I. "How about it? Let's go." Despite the cider-haze, I felt a yawning in the pit of my stomach.

An alleyway between what looked like warehouses led to a heavy door with a sliding panel. After some knocking the panel slid back, a woman's eyes surveyed our uniforms and the panel snapped shut. My relief was countered by renewed determination on the part of T. and Fish. They knocked insistently until the steps came back. This time Fish had a stream of imperfect French ready and after a bit the door creaked open.

The woman, wrinkled with thinning hair, led us to a dimly lit room with a bare wooden floor and tables and chairs in alcoves on either side. Opposite our table sat a French civilian in a dark suit with a girl in a plain dress. They stopped talking to look at us. The other alcoves were empty. Dance music played softly. It might have been a small village hall, got up for an occasion, just before the guests arrive.

Three girls came down steps at one end and walked towards us, unsmiling. They arranged chairs and sat down. The prettiest, who wore a dress and very little make-up, sat next to me; a slim rather intelligent-looking blonde, in tights and bra, next to T., and a large girl, with heavy bust, bulging thighs, dark short hair and a tight red mouth, next to Fish. Drinks were ordered and Fish, with his most charming, twitchy smile, tried to get a conversation going, without much success.

After a while he got up, came round to the girl in the dress next to me, gave a smiling bow and they made for the staircase. The other two rose. The blonde preceded T. The plump girl with the sour lips gave a quick blank glance over her shoulder to see that I was following. At the bottom of the stairs the wrinkled woman was waiting with packaged contraceptives. I climbed the stairs behind swinging hips and legs that suddenly looked elephantine. It was like walking in a dream you can't shake off.

All that registered of the room we entered was that it was very small, with a window facing a blank wall, a mirror, and a hard, clean bed, like a hospital bed. I stood facing the window, then glanced sideways into the mirror. The girl was unclipping her bra but then let her arms drop. She stood there, huge, inert, expressionless, waiting. I said suddenly, *"C'est impossible. Pardon, mais c'est impossible. J'ai une femme en Angleterre."*

I turned round. She looked at me briefly, with complete indifference, slightly shrugged and strained her plump arms behind her back to reclip the bra. I followed her downstairs and back to the table and asked if she would like a drink. She went

71

out and was followed back by Madame with beer and cognac for me and lemonade for her on a tray. Madame gave me a slight disapproving look but said nothing. We sat silent over the drinks, watching the Frenchman and his girl watching us.

T. came down first with the blonde and, over drinks, talked to her in a confidential undertone in English, which she could not understand and ignored. Fish came down holding hands with his girl. They were soon dancing together, gracefully cheek to cheek, the girl's eyes half-closed. The plump girl was by now sitting in another alcove with a new client, a tough middle-aged Frenchman who kept his beret on and looked quite at home.

We spent the night at a seaside resort south of Cherbourg at a small hotel where two prostitutes were holidaying. They really were on holiday and we saw them on the sandy beach next morning, in the scantiest of costumes, playing with a beach-ball with a group of young children, shouting and leaping and chasing like children themselves. The children obviously adored them and their mothers seemed smilingly content to have them off their hands for a bit and in such congenial company.

Back at Creully nothing had changed, nothing much had happened in our absence. Sir Archibald Sinclair, the Air Minister, was to open the first Malcolm Club in Europe at the Norman castle on Saturday. We had missed a roast chicken supper. They were still slogging it out south of Caen.

The typewriters started pounding again as, after more massive bombardments from the air, von Kluge's Seventh Army disintegrated into a rout through the Falaise Gap. All day from the airstrips around us Typhoons and Spitfires kept up a shuttle service of destruction along that narrow escape route to the Seine. Squadrons rivalled each other in their daily scores of vehicles, tanks and barges rocket-blasted or bombed. 'A Dunkirk in reverse' was the phrase to use for this ferocious mass onslaught on sitting targets.

I spent a day in the Gap with Rex North, columnist of the *Sunday Pictorial*, who had come over for the impending liberation of Paris.

"EAST OF FALAISE, WEDNESDAY.

"This is Typhoon territory. It stretches for miles along the roads east of Trun, diverging to take in here a farmyard and orchard, there the wooded banks of a stream. And the devastation within its boundaries beggars description.

"For a mile or two east of Trun the road runs through a countryside peaceful and beautiful as the Sussex Weald. Under a summer sky wheatfields and lush pastureland roll towards a blue horizon of wooded hills. War seems remote, unreal.

"Suddenly by the roadside the first signs of desolation appear. The ground is stained with the wreckage of a lorry – burned almost to cinders under the direct blast of a rocket.

"A few feet away a German youth sprawls in the ditch. He is staring up at the sky with blue and sightless eyes: his face frozen into terror, he lies like a grotesque and horrible waxwork.

"Here is the entry into a world of nightmare. From now on you must thread your way through the débris of a doomed retreat. What you had imagined from the stories of pilots lies here in terrible reality.

"From a POW cage into which dazed, dishevelled Germans are still pouring by the hundred, I followed a party back into the waste land. They were going to bury their dead. We came to a crossroads from which wreckage had been swept into ditches by our advancing troops and followed a lane to a farmhouse – now little more than rubble.

"In the yard and orchards around hundreds of vehicles, including tanks, had been assembled under camouflage. But our Typhoons had located them and with rockets and cannon-fire blasted them out of existence. It had been a strange assembly. Horse-drawn vehicles and guns predominated and dead horses lay grotesquely all around. Half-tracks, lorries and 'People's Cars' lay charred and wrecked beside hooded carts that might have come from a Wild West melodrama.

"The grass was littered with the loot of a master race turned rabble. There had been no half-measures in looting: wines, spirits, lace, silk stockings, perfume, oil paintings – I even saw babies' shoes, a train set, a tennis racket.

•

"Among the débris and in fields all round lay the German dead. A large barn, materially undamaged, had been converted into a German Red Cross centre: German and British doctors worked on the scores of wounded.

"Prisoners waiting to be taken in wandered about unescorted, searching the débris for valuable articles. The ground was strewn with rifles and ammunition. If there had been any fight left in them they could well have escaped. At one time I found myself in a field surrounded by some 50 Germans. So great was the evidence of complete demoralization that I had no qualms.

"In a corner of the farmyard a Polish captive was strumming a guitar, singing a melancholy song of his Fatherland. But he had more cause for happiness than many of the others. For there were many youths among these prisoners – youths who, having been deprived of faith in the Fuehrer, were left with no faith at all.

"This is only a segment of the great area of destruction that lies between Falaise and the Seine – a destruction which is still in progress. Our Typhoons and Spitfires have here revenged the massacres and atrocities of five years. The cup of retribution is brimming over."

Back at camp a message awaited me. I was being transferred to the Ninth Air Force, the American opposite number to 2nd TAF. Ronald Walker was coming to take over from me. I learned that there were twenty-one correspondents accredited to the Ninth, living in a damaged farmhouse and with only four jeeps between them. "Bad luck," said Rex. "You'll miss Paris."

Paris had seemed a tangible presence over the blue horizons of the Falaise Gap, crouched there expectant, waiting to leap into tumultuous life. I thought of that dreary farmhouse miles from anywhere, of the excited radio voices ("This is Paris!") as we slumped around, out of it all. I consulted Fish and T. T., who had turned down the Falaise trip as another 'waste of time', was not interested. Fish was. We teamed up with Rex and his photographer, Bill Turner, told the Information Officer that we were going on another recce-trip and set off.

Although the liberation of Paris was a notable exception to the generality that anticipation is better than realization, those two days approaching the resurgent city glow in the memory as no other time in the war. Mobbed by villagers who made no discrimination between uniforms, speeding down quiet roads where pockets of German resistance had lately been reported, nosing at last into the great concourse of troops and civilians tentatively but jubilantly converging on a capital now up in arms against its oppressors, was to feel the pulse of history, to ride on the crest of humanity's never-resolved conflict between good and evil – to be There.

On the afternoon of Friday, 25 August, I sat in a café with other correspondents trying to hammer from a typewriter an inkling of what it was like to be in a Paris gone frantic with joy. Despatch riders waited for the copy. The streets outside were in tumult. An American next to me slapped his palms against his temples. "It can't be done. You can't put this into words." The inadequacy of words hastily disgorged, emotion snuffed under cliché, was later painfully apparent. Not, in my case, publicly because my despatch was not used, whether as inadequate or repetitive of other *News Chronicle* correspondents with more right than I to a Paris dateline I never learned.

"The people of Paris, hysterical with joy, are crowding the streets outside this café south of the Seine. A few hundred yards north a nest of Germans is being rooted out: the crack of rifles and stutter of machine guns is a half-heard background to the cheering, the singing, the shouts of victory.

"No one seems to know how many Germans are still resisting and no one seems to care. French tanks, troops, gendarmerie, plough through milling crowds – crowds in whose eyes *joie de vivre* has been rekindled. Cars, jeeps and lorries lie marooned in seas of humanity: the faces of dust-grimed soldiers are ringed with lipstick, every vehicle is festooned with flowers.

"It has been a long, hard way into Paris – but now the welcome that has greeted our entry overwhelms all other thought. Four years of suppression have burst out today into a flood of ecstatic joy.

"Last night I celebrated the coming day of victory in a small village 12 miles south of Paris. For hours we had been probing the roads that lead to the capital, always to be turned back.

Although pockets of defence, in places strong, blocked our entry there were few signs of fighting. On roads ominously quiet and all but deserted a peasant or garage hand would wave us to a halt to warn of Germans lurking in the woods ahead.

"Towards nightfall we took the road from Rambouillet to approach Paris from the south-west. In every village and hamlet the tricolour was flying: the streets were lined with people, shouting, cheering, showering us with flowers, plying us with tomatoes. We were the first Englishmen many had seen in four years and their welcome was moving.

"We were halted some ten miles from the city. Tanks of General Leclerc's armoured column were bivouacked beside the roadway – from ahead came the rumble of guns. We found lodging for the night in a hotel, the White Horse. A banquet was being prepared. In the courtyard as we talked with villagers a young man in pin-striped trousers and open-necked shirt came to my side. "I suppose you're making for Paris," he said. The voice was unmistakably that of a Yorkshireman.

"The day after D-Day, navigating a Lancaster to a target south of Paris, he had been shot down. With him were three other RAF men, equally convincingly disguised. One of them, a Flight Lieutenant, had been in hiding for three months.

"We went in to dinner. In lamplight two long tables glittered with the food and wine of a great celebration. Village girls, rivals for the affections of the young airmen, members of the local Resistance back from a day's hunting of snipers, and soldiers of the F.F.I. sat down to the banquet. Wine flowed, spirits were unboundedly joyful. To their French protectors the RAF guests of honour were simply Max, Pierre, Jean, Arthur. Hundreds of pilots and bomber crews, they told us, are in hiding in Paris and the country around. And the day for which they have been waiting has come.

"After the food and wine came the songs. Everyone sang. All the village heard the Marseillaise and the National Anthem. We toasted the RAF, the Resistance Movement: we toasted the leaders of Free France, of Britain, America, Russia. It is a scene I shall not forget, this last stopping-place on the road to Paris.

"Early this morning we were on our way. It was a road that hundreds were taking. They came on foot, on bicycles, in ramshackle cars and country carts – the people of France returning to their capital. Ahead thundered the French tanks, behind came the men, women and children – the liberated and joyful people of France.

"Six miles from Paris a halt was called while the armour poured through. There was smoke on the horizon: a solitary Mosquito dived into the haze. But out of Paris came despatch riders: they told of fierce street battles north of the Seine: and they told also of a city gone mad with joy.

"Shortly after two o'clock the way to Paris was opened. Civilians, exhausted after journeying in many cases hundreds of miles, found a new burst of energy. On either side of the road they went forward – a fantastic, moving cavalcade.

"From the western suburbs onwards it has been a triumphal process. Children and girls have swarmed on to the roof of our car, shrieking with delight. The city rings with cries of 'Victoire!', 'Vive l'Angleterre!', 'Vive les Allies! Flags and flowers have strewn the path of our entry – and still it goes on.

"A mad, fantastic city, a city incredibly happy, incredibly generous in tribute. There is gunfire two blocks away. But the sounds of battle are indistinct in a pandemonium of joy and the armour of war is swallowed up in carnival crowds."

Later that afternoon, in the Hotel Scribe, which had appropriately been designated Press Headquarters and where correspondents from all over the free world were converging, looking variously elated or dazed by it all, I added a new intro for the spike.

"The blockades are up in the streets of Paris tonight. The spirit of the Revolution is abroad again: but today there is no civil war except for the collaborators. I have just seen one of the traitors of France – her head was shaved naked and gashed, she was dragged whimpering, her face crumpled in terror, in the centre of a crowd hysterical with the joy of liberation, the hatred of everything German.

"Fighting goes on in this city of fantastic contrasts. Crowds of many thousands are thronging the approaches to the Opera

House, while in the Place de la Concorde dug-in Tiger tanks maintain an intermittent, desperate fire. Our entry into the heart of Paris has been through streets clamorous with victory, tumultuous with crowds ecstatically gay. It has led us, too, past deserted streets, blocked at each end with barricades of sandbags and carts.

"Armed students and soldiers of the F.F.I. advance down these streets, their backs to the walls, while bullets ricochet from the pavement. In every house along these streets the shutters are up. Where a chink shows, you see here the face of a civilian trapped in his apartment, there the glint of a German helmet. In one broad boulevard I saw fate closing in on 200 S.S. men backed by five tanks. Behind the sandbags ambulances waited with engines running. A whiff of death stained the flower-perfumed air."

I spent four days in Paris, living mostly on champagne and spam, caught up in a carnival that scarcely abated even when the Luftwaffe indiscriminately showered the city with high explosive and incendiary bombs, killing over 100 civilians, two nights after our entry. Rex, Bill and I were the guests that night of a fashion designer at a dinner of an excellence that only the black market could have provided. Four of his models sat down with us in candlelight and, as the wine flowed, pidgin-English and pidgin-French provoked a merriment unheeding of the sudden crack of ack-ack guns, the clang of fire-engines, the crunch of a bomb.

"*Vous avez les yeux très belles*," I was trying out on the dark, twinkling Norwegian girl beside me when Rex, arm around a French blonde, called across the table in a voice of earnest determination, "How would you say 'Our meat ration is very small'?"

Invitations were thick on the ground at the Hotel Scribe. And one that I followed up with Bill enshrined these days of an unprecedented *entente cordiale*. We found ourselves outside a faded old house in Montparnasse. It looked either impenetrably blacked-out or lifeless. We rang and rang again. At last there came a shuffling down the passage and the door opened. A man in a dressing-gown, with a white, walrus-moustache, held up a candle to peer at us. We explained. He wrung our hands and welcomed us in, calling excitedly up the stairs into a darkness imposed by the absence of electricity and a shortage of candles.

But candles are stuck liberally now in a room with crowded bookshelves, romantic water-colours, an upright piano, and figures emerge into the soft glow from the outer darkness, all in dressing-gowns. There is walrus-moustache's wife, matronly and smiling, his pretty, shy young daughter, a Polish lady, once beautiful, a faded spinster who is ushered, all coyness, from the shadows to be introduced as a valiant member of the Resistance.

Our host goes out to return with two bottles of vintage champagne, hoarded throughout the Occupation, he says, for just this occasion. We play the role of liberators as toast after toast is drunk, emotionally at attention. He is very proud of his Scottish ancestry and I rack my brains in vain for a famous Scotsman to propose, making do with *'L'Ecosse!'* After an exchange of personal experiences during the past days, the Polish lady is drawn to the piano. She plays Chopin and I watch her once-beautiful face.

I am asked if I play and admit to doing so badly, and only from music. Beethoven's sonatas are produced and I fumble through the first two movements of the 'Moonlight', while the pretty daughter holds a candle over me, dripping grease on the keys. She produces music for four hands and sits to the right of me on the stool. She plays far better than I and laughs encouragingly when my right hand gets caught up with her left. Her father and Bill, both professing an allergy to music, sit in a corner talking animatedly about Pétain.

It is after midnight, the bottles are empty, the last vestige of ice broken, but we must go. They accompany us to the door, with candles, and say that we must return without fail. *'Musique pour les quatre mains!'* I call towards two dark eyes behind a flame. But we do not return.

On the third day Rex tore himself away from the beautiful stately model he had got Bill to pose for the *Sunday Mirror* on her bicycle in the Champs Elysées as a symbol of La Belle France resurgent and who had fallen for his lean and hungry looks, to accompany me to a plain-looking building that had been the Ministry of the Interior. The Gendarme officer who showed us round suggested we should try to imagine ourselves as members of the Resistance as he explained the Procedure.

In that narrow cupboard in a corner of the entrance hall we would first be locked up with some half dozen others, with scarcely room to breathe, for a period long enough to make us want to scream to be let out. We would be taken out one by one, stripped naked and beaten. Truncheons made of rubber, iron filings or sand, are still littered around. We would then put on our clothes and be left to our thoughts.

For the next stage the officer led us upstairs to a large, carpeted room, with easy chairs, a swivel chair by a capacious desk and oil paintings on the walls. Here we would have been seated opposite a quite benevolent-seeming Gestapo officer, who might commiserate on the rough handling we had received and give his word that nothing of that sort would happen to us again if we were sensible enough to cooperate. He would have a file in front of him and make it clear that he knew too much about us for lying to be of any avail.

It was a room that the benevolent Gestapo officer had evidently been loath to vacate. The leather upholstery of the chairs had been ripped so that the hair stuffing oozed through the gashes. The oil paintings, nondescript though they were, had been slashed. Even the typewriter on the secretary's table had been hammered into a wreck.

The officer then led us up the two flights we might have been required to climb had we declined to be sensible. Wooden steps led to what at first glance might have been the cheerless attic bathroom in the maids' quarters of a Victorian home. Then we noticed that above the stark bath-tub was a pulley with cords dangling. Immersion of the head at regular intervals into icy water, said the officer, was a particularly productive torture.

Down in a courtyard a bonfire had been made of a great pile of identity cards, on one side two head-and-shoulder photographs, in profile and full-face, on the other the prisoner's name, description and brief history. Most had been burned to ash but on the perimeter some had escaped the flames. I picked one out and pocketed it.

"*MONTARELLO, Raphael, né le 29 novembre 1917 à Radicena (It.), fils de Roche et de Marmollite Therese. Mandat d'arrêt du 26 avril 1944 de M. Florens, J.I. à Aix-en-Provence. Inculpé d'évasion, port d'arme, menaces de mort.*
"*SIGNALEMENT. Taille 1 m. 67, cheveux châtaine, front fuyant, nez rectiligne, teint clair.*
"*RENSEIGNEMENTS. Ajusteur, demeurant à L'Estaque. Figure sue la circ. 62/44 U avec photo.*"

Raphael Montarello is wearing a sports jacket and open-neck shirt. In profile he has his head held up, mouth drawn down. In full face his dark hair is seen sleekly smoothed back from a low forehead. His dark eyebrows curve up above the nose, screwing up the eyes so that the pupils gaze out from half-closed lids, dark pupils that reflect either pain or anticipation of pain. His mouth looks as though it is closed on clenched teeth. What became of him I do not know.

That afternoon we went to the Paris Prefecture to see some of the 500 collaborators so far arrested, some 20 per cent of them women. One of the chief collaborators was led into the room between two hustling gendarmes. His face had been used as a punchbag, eyes glinting through puffs of flesh, lips swollen and flecked with caked blood, cheeks ballooned and raw. The officer recited a summary of his crimes and snapped at him for an admission of guilt. He said nothing, swaying slightly. The gendarmes prodded him. He still said nothing. We indicated that we were satisfied.

On the way out, after an interview with a senior official, we were taken into a room full of women, sitting on benches or standing around. A few had head-scarves but most were bare-headed, literally so. The gendarme in charge singled out three for our inspection. One had a black scarf clutched round her head. It was whisked away to reveal the scalp, bald as an egg. I did not register the summary of their crimes. Two looked like high-class prostitutes. One was flauntingly unrepentant. As the gendarme read her name, she put her hands on her hips, waggling them and drew her unpainted lips into a leer.

She threw back her head as we left, but there was no hair to make that gesture effective.

Outside the Café de la Paix you watched the patriotic girls go by, aloof or smiling on bicycles, dressed, despite all the rigours of occupation, to kill. I sat there on the fourth day discussing our departure with Fish, who had been off on his own for most of the time. We were suddenly hailed. It was a senior Information Officer from Creully.

There had been something of a hue and cry for us, it appeared. An urgent message awaited me at Creully and Fish too was wanted. I said I had been staying at the Hotel Scribe, presumably with the full knowledge of my office, having filed three stories after my first despatch. (I later found that those on the Luftwaffe raid and the Gestapo headquarters had been used, though cut.) Better surely, I suggested, than kicking my heels in a Ninth Air Force outpost. "You'd better get back quick," said the Information Officer. "I think there's trouble."

Fish drove back fast. Most of the tents were down and most of the correspondents gone. A letter awaited from Ronald Walker:

"I am very sorry that you did not wait to see me, particularly in view of the developments which have taken place. Apart from the fact that you were ordered to the Ninth Air Force on my arrival and have not done so, thereby seriously embarrassing my position here, the D.P.R. has informed me that you have got yourself into a serious jam over some incident around Cherbourg. A report has come through the American military police and it is being taken up at high level.

"As this camp is moving and you have not put in an appearance, I have given instructions that you, as my assistant, are to be returned to London. The Editor has been informed and your move to the Ninth Air Force will be dealt with in London."

T. was still in the camp. "What are you going to do about it?" Fish asked. T. looked pained. "Me? I told you you were fools to give your names."

CHAPTER NINE

Back in war-weary, bomb-battered, but still indomitable London, not even the shadow of the pending high-level investigation into that 'incident near Cherbourg' could dim the reflected glory of one of the very few 'I-was-there' stories that everybody wanted to know about.

In Fleet Street pubs this occasionally took an embarrassing wink-wink-nudge-nudge turn, reminding me of the comment I had overheard from an American warco that first chaotic night at the Hotel Scribe: "Anybody who doesn't sleep with a woman tonight is just an exhibitionist." The popular press had made much of the astonishingly chic appearance of the average Parisienne, an example splashed in the *Sunday Pictorial* being the glamorous model photographed by Bill Turner in the Champs Elysées, about whose love-making finesse Rex North had so gloatingly enthused.

In such a context my *'Musique pour les quatre mains'* and two dark eyes behind a candle flame were best kept to myself. I was on securer ground displaying one of the coshes I had found left behind at the Gestapo headquarters, a canvas-covered monstrosity weighted with iron filings, or telling of the macho carryings-on of Ernest Hemingway, who, discarding his war correspondent insignia and armed to the teeth, had led two truck-loads of resistance fighters to 'liberate' the Ritz Hotel in the Place Vendôme, demanding of the barman, "How about forty-seven dry martinis?"

At the *News Chronicle* Gerald Barry, putting on a stern front in his sanctum, started by saying that the 'serious jam' I had got myself into, as reported to him by Ronnie Walker, was up to me to clear up and he didn't want to know anything about it. What did concern him was the disruption I had caused by disobeying orders. As one of Fleet Street's most liberally minded and cultured of editors (knighted after the war for his services as Director General of the Festival of Britain), I had a feeling that, with Paris the lure, he would have done exactly as I had done had he been in my shoes. "You're doing some good work,' he concluded, "but don't get big-headed."

From Fish I learned that the Saturday after our return had been fixed for a tribunal hearing, and that it would be presided over by the Deputy Director Public Relations at the Air Ministry, Lord Willoughby de Broke, a name that rang no bell with me except an alarm one. It seemed that the American M.P.'s complaints against us had indeed been inflated into something of a test case on Anglo-American relations.

In the five months leading up to D-Day an additional three-quarters of a million Yanks had arrived in Britain, bringing the total to one and a half million, and it was common knowledge that, to the British Tommy, with only a quarter of their basic pay and nothing approaching the largesse of their camps, they were more than ever seen as objects of envy, even hostility – "over-paid, over-fed, over-sexed and over here." Transferred to the battlefield such hostility could have serious consequences, though, as Fish pointed out, it was stretching it a bit to pick on the case of a half-pissed British warco telling an American 'snowball' to 'push off, sonny boy'.

In the event the occasion proved a good deal less of an ordeal than anticipated. This was partly because the amount of celebratory drinking engendered by the liberation of Paris had induced a relaxed sense of well-being, partly because I felt that I had nothing much to feel guilty about. (Mercifully the gate-crashing of an out-of-bounds brothel had gone undetected.)

I kept no record of that Saturday morning tribunal, and my recollections of it are hazy: of being escorted from the entrance hall of the semi-deserted Air Ministry along echoing corridors to a door, through which Fish was first ushered, while I waited outside, dimly hearing the rise and fall of voices, until he emerged some little time later, greeting me with one of his twisted smiles and a thumbs up sign, and it was my turn.

My memory is of taking a seat opposite three uniformed officers behind a desk, the middle one of whom (presumably Lord Willoughby de Broke) did most of the questioning, in a tone suggesting that Fish had effectively left me in the clear. I had already made up my mind not to implicate the absent T., and the fact that, after repeated questioning, I declined to do so clearly went in my favour. The code of the Old School Tie held. I had owned up to my misdeeds but had not committed the cardinal sin of sneaking or blabbing, even against a character so obviously not only a cad but a coward. "Thank you for your frank answers," Lord Willoughby concluded. "I think you may now get on with the rest of your war!"

It had occurred to me at the time that it was peculiarly insensitive of the Americans not to have turned a blind eye on an incident that involved a former Battle of Britain pilot, one of the Few to whom so many (including the then-isolationist Americans) had owed so much. But it was not until many years later, in reading the fifth volume of Winston Churchill's history of the Second World War, that I discovered what a role Lord Willoughby de Broke had played at that time, and how he must have felt at being required to pass judgement on a member of that exclusive fraternity.

On what became known as Battle of Britain Day, 15 September, 1940, the day that the Luftwaffe made its most concentrated daylight attack but suffered such losses that Hitler's invasion plans were finally abandoned, Churchill drove from Chequers to No 11 Fighter Group headquarters at Uxbridge to see the outcome in the theatre-like underground Operations Room.

After describing at length the setting, procedures and progress of that history-making occasion, he comes to the final phase: "The Air Vice-Marshal gave general directions for the disposal of his fighter force, which were translated into detailed orders to each Fighter Station by a staff officer in the centre of the 'Dress Circle', at whose side I sat. Some years later I asked his name. He was Lord Willoughby de Broke. (I met him next in 1947, when the Jockey Club, of which he was a steward, invited me to see the Derby.) He now gave orders for the individual squadrons to ascend and patrol, as the result of the final information which appeared on the map-table."

Had I known that at the time I would have found it hard to believe that an officer who had played such a pivotal role in what Churchill described as a battle as decisive as Waterloo should, four years later, have me in his sights while deliberating on a matter of such trifling import. Such were the vagaries of war. To Fish, let off with a mild reprimand for breaking bounds, it was all a bit of a joke, to be taken in his stride, as he took most things.

In Warwick Square my return from France, in an RAF car driven by Fish, had been an occasion for effusive celebration in Mrs Monckton's ground floor flat, where it took little time for her to respond to his devil-may-care charm. Fish afterwards pronounced her 'quite a dish', and it came as no great surprise when I later got from him that he had returned more than once to her flat when I was away on an assignment, and described her in terms that had never entered my head, even during that protracted game of blind-man's-bluff at Anne's Christmas party.

The assignment came out of the blue, a week after the tribunal, and the fact that I was not in the office when news of it arrived added another minor blot to my copybook. At a loose end while awaiting a decision on my next accreditation, I had become bored sitting at my desk doing nothing and it was not until late afternoon that I looked in, to find there had been another hue and cry. So it was that I boarded a train at Waterloo next morning, bearing a missive from a Wing Commander B. Sprigg, Public Relations Division, Supreme Headquarters, Allied Expeditionary Force, addressed to the Officer Commanding RAF Station, Tarrant Rushton:

"The bearer of Air Ministry Pass No 19488, Mr M. Moynihan of the *News Chronicle*, was unable to report in time to accompany the Press Party which left for Tarrant Rushton yesterday on special assignment. He is therefore proceeding separately by train, as arranged with F/Lt. Evans, and it is requested that he may be given the same facilities that are being extended to the other accredited Press Correspondents who reported to your Station yesterday."

An example of the meticulous bumph that attended our every move, this was at least justified on security grounds, though the note of urgency proved misplaced. It was not for eight days after my arrival at the sprawling airfield near Blandford Forum in Dorset that the 'special assignment' took off, and not until the day before that we learned precisely what it was.

From the lines of gliders and tow-planes crowding the hangars and runways, the nature of the forthcoming operation was immediately apparent, and we correspondents had ample time to gather background information. Since the Allied breakthrough from Normandy, we learned, glider and tug pilots at airfields across southern and eastern England had been on constant alert. Time and again they had been briefed, aircraft fuelled and gliders loaded with equipment for fancily named operations ('Linnet', 'Axehead', 'Infatuate') which had been called off at the last moment, largely because of the unexpected speed of the Allied advance. After the liberation of Paris, newspaper headlines had exulted in the tally of towns falling like ninepins – Amiens, Verdun, Arras, Liège, Brussels, Antwerp, Maastricht – but now what remained of von Rundstedt's beaten army were at bay, backs to their Siegfried Line on the borders of Germany, and a stalemate was in prospect.

It was to prevent this that General Montgomery had devised an audacious plan, code-named Market Garden, aimed at bringing the war to a speedy conclusion by surrounding the vital 400-square-mile industrial area of the Ruhr. To achieve this 9,000 Allied paratroops and 1,100 glider crews were to be dropped along a 60-mile front to secure five major bridges across the Rhine for ground troops to cross over. It would be the task of the First British Airborne Division to capture the northernmost of these bridges, at a Dutch town called Arnhem.

Kept in the dark about all this, we passed the time in accumulating information unlikely to make copy but worth knowing. Combat gliders, we learned, were colloquially known as 'flying coffins', and with good reason. The Germans had been the first to use them, during their invasion of Crete in 1941, but their losses had been so great that they had confined their use thereafter to carrying freight. For the British, their first

87

use, in the invasion of Sicily in 1943, had been equally disastrous, a night operation entailing a four-hour sea crossing which ended with 379 men killed or wounded and 326 men 'missing presumed drowned'.

It had been a different story four months ago, when over 8,000 glider troops had played a crucial role in helping consolidate the D-Day landings, with comparatively light casualties. But to the glider pilots I talked to, a number of whom had been in that operation, it was still fingers crossed for the next one. To be towed into action over enemy territory in such a flimsy contraption, and, on release from the towing cable, to glide soundlessly to earth, looking out for trees and other obstacles to avoid before crash-landing, was, as one phlegmatic pilot put it, 'somewhat dicey'.

As a reaction to the tension, evenings in the Mess tended to end in boozy sing-songs, ranging from the maudlin to the scatological, of which two choruses, belted out at full throttle, come to mind:

A nursery rhyme tune was the setting for the first:

> "Oh dear what can the matter be
> Three old ladies locked in the lavatory
> They have been there from Monday to Saturday
> Nobody knows they are there ... "

John Peel provided lift-off for the second:

> "Cats on the rooftops
> Cats on the tiles
> Cats with syphilis
> Cats with piles
> Cats with their a-a-arse ho-o-oles
> Wreathed in smiles
> As they revelled in the joys of fornication."

Even a strict security clampdown on the airfield, and a preliminary briefing the day before the operation, failed to quell all sounds of revelry, and not a few hangovers were being regretted next morning when more detailed briefings confirmed that there was to be no cancellation this time. This was the Big One.

To a British public impatient for action, the morning of Monday, 18 September brought news to lift the spirits. "Montgomery to his troops last night – the triumphant cry now is 'Forward into Germany,' " proclaimed the *News Chronicle* above a banner headline, 'Airborne Army Seizes Towns in Holland'. Down the page the first of my three despatches was headed 'Diary of the Allies' greatest airborne operation'.

"This was an army in flight. Flight not in the German sense, for we were headed towards Holland. From horizon to horizon the sky was alive with Allied aircraft: Dakotas carrying paratroops, Halifaxes and Stirlings towing gliders weighted with men and material. The greatest airborne operation in history was under way.

"The Dutch coast appeared through a warm haze. To the men of the First Airborne Army it was the promised land. Within 45 minutes they would be in action on enemy-held soil. Long training, months of dogged practice, interminable dress rehearsals, lay behind: ahead action awaited, the real thing.

"The full story of this historic operation cannot yet be told. My story is confined to one airfield among the many from which the airborne armada took off, and on that airfield to one plane. M for Mike is the Halifax from which I witnessed this stupendous undertaking. Our job was to tow a Hamilcar, the world's biggest glider, deep into occupied territory. Our freight consisted of two Bren-gun carriers, our 'passengers' five North Country men of the Airborne Army.

"It was over a week ago that I came to this airfield in the West Country, but not until yesterday did Operation Market Garden become a reality. At 11 in the morning the camp was sealed. Sentries guarded its boundaries. The bus service to the local town was cancelled. In all parts of the camp preparations were made. Halifax crews went over their charts and maps with a thoroughness that could leave no room for mistakes.

"At six o'clock this morning the sleeping camp was roused for its great day. On the runways two long rows of Horsas and Hamilcars waited, the latter already filled with their equipment

– carriers, guns, light tanks. Glider and tug pilots were given a final briefing. The Group Captain read a message from the A.O.C. wishing pilots and crews all luck in this great mission. In the warm autumn sunshine of this fourth anniversary of the Battle of Britain, troops and crews stood beside the giant machines that were soon to take them into action. They joked over cups of tea laced with rum, chalked the names of girl friends on the sides of their gliders.

"At the end of the long column of aircraft M for Mike waited beside a Hamilcar that bore the macabre inscription – 'The undertaker and his stiffs'. We were the 13th and last of the Hamilcar towers. At 10.50 we taxied to the long runway. At 10.53 we were airborne. This is the diary I made of an historic flight:

"11.45. We are flying in a blue sky, cloudless except for aircraft – and what an exception! On our starboard side, front and behind the armada stretches. M for Mike is not standing up well to the strain of the 15 tons dead weight behind. The other 12 Hamilcars have outdistanced us. The pilot and navigator decide to cut off a loop in our course to make up time. We are off now on our own. 2,000 feet below people are coming out of country churches and staring up in wonder.

"12.15. Approaching the coast the navigator says, 'I have cut off as much as I can, but we are going to be hellishly late.'

"1.15. We are over Holland. From the bomb-aimer's turret in the nose I see a flooded countryside, the water is still and looks like green slime from which rooftops, trees and telegraph poles protrude. First of the fighter escort sighted – Mosquitoes hedge-hopping below us, Spitfires above.

"1.20. First signs of life below: groups of civilians staring up from country roads and village greens.

"1.30. Scores of Dakotas are passing to our starboard – on the way home. This is the Continent, but it seems to be 'traffic on the left'. None of the flak areas have been active.

"1.55. This is it. 'OK boys, I'm casting off now,' comes the glider pilot's voice. 'Thanks for the lift.' They're away.

"Below the fields north of the Rhine are cluttered with gliders. To port there is a wonderful spectacle as the Dakotas disgorge their troops. The sunlit area is bright with parachutes. The fighting seems to have moved west. Smoke rises from the woods and a large area of gorse is on fire. I see 'the undertaker' touching down among the litter of gliders, a perfect landing.

"2.00. Headed for home. We have climbed above clouds and seem to be all alone in this remote upper world. For fighters or flak we have been all along and still are a sitting target. But the enemy appears to have been thoroughly stunned!"

"19 September. The invasion by airborne troops behind the German lines in Holland continued this afternoon without interference. For the second time within 24 hours I flew to within a few miles of the German border: apart from a few bursts of flak, there was no evidence that the countryside below was enemy occupied.

"Halifax pilots and crews at this station, most of them veterans of Bomber Command or Coastal Command, have been amazed and even disappointed at the uneventfulness of this stupendous operation. On maps in the Operations Room the course over Holland threads its way through red crayon rings, indications of major flak areas. Intelligence had warned that in one area alone 240 light and 60 heavy ack ack guns were massed.

"The western approaches to Holland were at one time the most heavily defended in Europe. Pilots have told me that, flying on bombing missions over these areas a year ago, they had run the gauntlet of flak even at 18,000 feet. Today, with a few exceptions, the airborne penetrations into Holland have been as uneventful as a large-scale exercise.

"In the co-pilot's seat of F for Freddie, a Halifax towing a Hamilcar, I could see a great fleet of aircraft stretching on all sides, a mammoth ferry service bringing more men and more material for the final assault on the Reich. Over the still dark waters of the North Sea their shadows were like moving arrows, headed inexorably towards Hitler's European fortress.

"As far as the eye could see the Dutch islands were wastes of watery desolation – flooded some two months ago against invasion by sea. There was grim irony in the flight of an airborne army above the waterlogged landscape. Two minutes after crossing the coast we were greeted by bursts of heavy flak to starboard. It was the only flak we encountered, and the flak ship from which it came was soon wreathed in smoke and flame, silenced by rocket-firing Typhoons.

"At 2.40 we reached our objective. Our Hamilcar joined other gliders circling down to the fields on which yesterday's fleet were clustered by the hundred. From a number of points on the landing-strip white smoke appeared: it was evident that they were still under enemy fire. Fires burned in some houses beside a railway whose sides were pitted with craters.

"On the return journey I searched the countryside for evidence of enemy occupation. But, although civilians on foot and on bicycles were fairly numerous on the roads, I saw no uniformed German and not a single vehicle. For hundreds of square miles Holland seemed to be a peaceable country, unencumbered with occupying troops. The 750-mile trip was indeed so unexceptionable that one might have thought at times that a fleet of peacetime airliners, not a fleet of war planes, darkened the skies."

"20 September. Across Belgium – the liberated areas and the areas where British troops are still locked in battle – an airborne fleet, the third instalment of a winged army, thundered this afternoon towards the landing strip in Holland.

"To the troops of the Second Army the flight of the great armada over the battlefield must have been an inspiring spectacle: to the battered and retreating Germans the effect on morale can only be guessed.

"For two days the airborne troops had been flown across Holland. Today they followed a new course. From 2,500 feet I hoped for a dramatic close-up of our front-line troops and of the villages and towns of Belgium and Southern Holland, some recently liberated, some still awaiting liberation, on my third flight to the landing strip. But third time was unlucky.

"My vantage point was the co-pilot's seat of M for Mike, the Halifax from which I saw the first stage of this unparalleled operation. M for Mike had already revealed a tendency towards unorthodox behaviour. On Sunday we had reached the landing strip alone, 30 minutes behind the main stream. Today an accident which might have proved fatal to our glider turned us back with our mission unfulfilled.

"In reading of the clockwork precision and the all but perfect timing of this great airborne operation, the difficulties and hazards faced by our glider pilots and tug crews have perhaps been minimized. Today, in carrying reinforcements to Holland, they have had to battle against appalling weather conditions. Good visibility is essential for glider towing. To run into cloud, if only for a few seconds, can be fatal. It was so in our case.

"Although at briefing we had been promised a reasonably high cloud ceiling, it was evident as we approached the East Coast that we were in for a difficult passage. As we roared out to sea in the midst of a great stream of troop and transport aircraft, grey mists closed around us. Ahead I could see our formation of Halifaxes and Horsas silhouetted against the mist, an awe-inspiring spectacle. At times the mist thinned. It was like the drawing of a curtain as aircraft, scores of them, were seen to be all around us.

"Such glimpses, however, were brief. The mist thickened and Flt Lieut Don Lee brought us down to 500 feet in an attempt to avoid the thicker patches. Even at such low an altitude ships were only just visible. The rest of the armada were invisible companions. It was an anxious time. Apart from the necessity of keeping visual control between tug and glider the possibility of collision in so thick a stream of aircraft loomed up.

"The 15 minutes between which we crossed and recrossed the Belgian coast were the most dramatic in the 15 hours I have spent in the air during the past three days. I quote from notes I scrawled in the third instalment of an airborne diary.

"2.10. Approaching the coast. Can see tall hotels on the seafront. We are down to 400 feet, but visibility is still very bad. Glider pilot is warned to look out for our rear Aldis. Thicker cloud envelops us. Across the docks now – there are signs of shelling. By the coast there are a number of concrete forts and gun emplacements.

"2.15. We're running into thick cloud. Don calls, 'I am going down. Show the red!' The rear gunner is shouting to glider pilot, 'Steady, glider, steady. To starboard, get to starboard.' His voice rises. 'Take care!' There's a snap like the crack of a whip and M for Mike lurches forward – released. The Horsa has gone.

"2.20. Horsa sighted, two fields from the church and school of a village. We pass over. A crowd has already collected round it. The port wing is splintered, but the crew are out and seem all right.

"2.30. We have made four circuits round the Horsa, avoiding chimneys and the church tower as we circle low over the field. A flock of seagulls flies into us – three dull thuds like flak. By the fourth time a huge crowd has surrounded the glider, including several Tommies. The glider pilot stands on the nose and waves his scarf as we turn for home.

"2.40. We are above the cloud under a blue sky. The rear gunner explains that the glider pilot lost sight of us in the mist. He saw the tow-rope suddenly sag to port as the glider dropped. As he pulled, the pilot tried to right himself, but too abruptly. The terrific strain snapped the thick rope like cotton. Don says, 'It makes you sick to hear the rope go like that.'

"The sun is blinding; the cloud tops are incredibly beautiful. But we all feel bitter about the way things have turned out. The safety of the Horsa is some consolation.

"So we came home. Another Halifax followed us – its glider had met the same fate. But despite the weather, which over the Belgian coast forced many tugs down as low as 50 feet, only four gliders from this station failed to reach their objective. One was shot down by heavy flak, another was cut loose when flak, by a million-to-one chance, severed the rope."

By the time I got back to London it was clear that Monty's gamble was not coming off, and that what had been billed as a second D-Day, backed by his confident assertion that the war would be over by the end of the year, had become a second Dunkirk, all that mattered now being how many of our beleaguered troops could escape to fight another day. The Home Front atmosphere was perfectly caught by the American journalist Mollie Panter-Downes, whose regular 'London War

Notes' in the *New Yorker* gave such a refreshingly objective viewpoint:

"This past week everybody's attention was painfully fixed on Arnhem. Words of any kind were difficult to utter and countless English families paid the story of the courageous stand at Arnhem the tribute of saying absolutely nothing as they sat at their radios listening to the tired broadcasters who had come to tell what had happened. The story of Arnhem, which already has become a proud part of English history, was being read to school children before the week was out. Even though people had gone around for weeks saying that the battle would get tough when it got near Germany, it was a jolt when they realized how right they had been."

Ben Fleming's involvement with the war, except as it directly affected him, had been minimal, as befitted a James Joycean 'Irishman in exile', and, though he and Carola were avid for news of Paris when we met (Carola had been an art student there for a year before the war), my officer's uniform proved something of a barrier to the old intimacy when we met on our own.

One of these occasions was a lunchtime session at the King's Head and Eight Bells, my favourite Chelsea pub, not far from Ben's digs in Oakley Street. Glimpsed through its windows, sunshine glowed on the autumnal trees along the Thames embankment, and sunshafts lit drifts of tobacco smoke in the uncrowded saloon bar, where, at a table near us, Dylan Thomas held court to the usual hangers-on.

When we arrived he was in the middle of a literary parlour game of his own devising, which consisted of someone naming a nursery rhyme, another a well-known writer, the challenge to Dylan being to recite that nursery rhyme in the style of that writer. Although, as we learned later, he was surfacing for the second time from a prolonged drinking bout, his rendition of Three Blind Mice as an addition to T.S. Eliot's *Waste Land* and Henry James's convoluted version of Little Jack Horner came out, after a concentrated silence, to brilliant effect.

Ben listened to all this with rapt attention, and, when Dylan had had enough, fumbled in his pockets for pen and paper and, to my amazement, crossed over to ask if he might have Dylan's autograph, 'for a friend'. The Welsh bard reacted favourably to this bow-tied, corduroy-jacketed Irishman, even more so to his "What will you be drinking?", and I was soon seated at the table beside a Ben I could scarcely recognize, sycophantically eulogizing Dylan on a recently broadcast poetry reading of his.

I had earlier noted Dylan glancing across at our table and registering disapproval at my uniform and shoulder flashes, and it was doubtless this, coupled with Ben's behaviour, that prompted me to say that I much preferred the stories about his Welsh childhood in *Portrait of the Artist as a Young Dog* to his poetry.

Disapproval turned to disgust as Dylan glared across at me and launched into a character assassination – my uniform and all it stood for, my warco status, the way I puffed at my pipe, unlike (he demonstrated) the quick motions of a cigarette smoker, my voice, which he found some difficulty in effectively mimicking as being too growly, his own voice being famous for its belly-deep reverberance.

Of the rest of the session I have no recollection except that, at some stage, Dylan turned to the lean-faced man sprawled in a chair beside him, slowly ran fingers along his crotch, and boomed, "You know I think I'd really fancy you if I was that way inclined," a gesture quite evidently meant to shock.

Only later did it occur to me that it could have been to impress Carola that Ben had inveigled himself into Dylan's company, the Bohemian anti-establishment rebel par excellence. They saw eye to eye with each other on most things connected with the arts (Picasso and Corbusier their current icons) and, more suprisingly, on political issues. Carola's left-wing leanings struck me as strangely at odds with her upper class background. The daughter of a Brigadier, she had had a debutante's upbringing, ending with a year at a Swiss finishing school and a short-lived marriage to the ex-Etonian son of Sir Harry Luke, Governor of the Fiji Islands, and for some months after her divorce had stayed in the palatial Ottawa residence of her favourite Aunt Susie (alias the aristocratic Lady Tweedsmuir) and her uncle,

Lord Tweedsmuir, Governor-General of Canada (alias John Buchan).

It was of John Buchan I immediately thought when Carola invited me to a small party at the Mayfair flat of her widowed mother, who, with the recently widowed Lady Tweedsmuir, was coming up from her Wendover farm to meet Ben, and where she would particularly like me to meet one of her closest friends, Elizabeth Wheller, a sweet girl whom she knew I would like.

As preparation I dipped again into the 1,204 pages of one of my favourite school prizes, *The Four Adventures of Richard Hannay*, at the heart of it a breathless description of General Hannay's last-ditch stand during the German offensive of 1918, during which Peter Pienaar, the grizzled old hero from his South African days, intercepts the Hun's ace pilot Lensch as, carrying vital information, he flies back to his lines, and, to make sure of a kill, crashes into him. As a 14-year-old I had revelled in that tear-jerking, Kamikaze-type encounter ("Somewhere up in the void two heroes were fighting their last battle"), and still found it hard to resist.

In the event Richard Hannay got no mention at the party, where Ben was the centre of attention and I only briefly met the charming Aunt Susie, and where I was standing, pipe in hand, with my back to the fire when a voice said, "I always think of an Englishman with his back to the fire smoking a pipe". Sweet was the right word for Carola's friend Lisa, instantly likeable, warm and outgoing, in almost every way the opposite to that mysterious, elusive Not Impossible She of my adolescent dreams.

I had now received my marching orders – the American Ninth Army, only recently arrived on the Continent, whose headquarters and press camp were in the process of being established at a Dutch town called Maastricht – and Lisa and I only twice met again. We swopped family and personal backgrounds: I impressed her with a purchase I had just made, on office expenses, from Simpsons of Piccadilly, an exorbitantly priced sheepskin coat to guard against the Ardennes winter: she made me solemnly promise that I would keep a diary until we met again.

CHAPTER TEN

"Thursday, 19 October, 1944. Hotel Scribe, Paris.

"At six o'clock yesterday evening I returned to Paris. It is seven weeks ago today that I left a city where jubilation, so delirious on the day we entered, was only just dying down. Now all is different. The new Occupation – of the Allied troops – has passed the stage of novelty. People go about their business as in any city, with private preoccupations, no longer turning to stare after a khaki uniform, no longer a community in rejoicing."

The first few pages of the diary I kept until the German breakthrough in the Ardennes two months later are wholly devoted to Paris, written in a way that underlines a factor not generally recognized. For the great majority of men serving overseas in the Second World War, for whom pre-war holidays had usually meant nothing more than a week or two at the nearest seaside resort, the very fact of being abroad was an adventure. My only foreign venture had been that fortnight's school expedition to Germany in 1936, thrilling beyond belief. Now, in the company of correspondents mostly a good deal older and accustomed to travel, I felt constrained to act blasé. The diary was an outlet for my true feelings.

"From our Dakota, which brought us rather bumpily through intermittent cloud over the Channel and Normandy, we had a magnificent view of Paris in the radiance of an autumnal sunset. Flying directly over the Eiffel Tower, we could see all the famous buildings on either side of the coiling Seine, substantial in the orange light. No city could have looked squalid in such a light. Paris, beautiful in symmetry and setting, took one's breath.

"There were nine of us in this Dakota, including an American warco also en route for the Ninth Army, Ned Roberts of

United Press. At the airfield a bus waited to drive us into Paris. Dusk was deepening in the suburbs – people hurrying home with briefcase or shopping bag, queueing for the few buses that now run, putting up shop shutters, counting money, grouped around the curving bar of a café: humdrum to its citizens, romantic to anyone for whom the word Paris has from childhood glowed like no other, a city so familiar to the imagination, here amazingly real and around.

"The crowded streets of suburbs give place to broad boulevards, where the leaves of trees glitter in artificial light and huge buildings loom against the pale sky. Over the massive bulk of Notre Dame I saw a star shine and was caught up in a whirl of half-remembered fantasies – Héloïse and Abélard, the Hunchback, *A Tale of Two Cities*, *The Scarlet Pimpernel*. Over Notre Dame bridge, the waters of the Seine, pale on one side, dark on the other, we passed the Louvre, the golden equestrian statue of Joan of Arc, then along the Rue de Rivoli with glimpses of elegant bars, world-famous hotels. From the Hotel Vendome, where the bus deposited us, a porter preceded Ned and myself with our luggage to the Scribe.

"On the way up to our rooms Ned met an American acquaintance who followed us up with two girls and a bottle of Armagnac. The conversation was pidgin sex and I left it after a while to see who was in the bar. SHAEF recently moved over here from London and the Scribe is even fuller of correspondents than in the hectic days of the liberation, when typewriters pounded among the popping of corks and the distant staccato of bullets. It is organized now, efficient and tame. In the course of the evening I drank with Norman Clark, Vernon Bartlett, Alan Tompkins, Stanley Bishop, met two others bound for the Ninth (*Times* and *Chicago Tribune*), ended up with cognac in Iris Carpenter's room."

A solo sightseeing tour the following day, with frequent 'seeing-the-world-go-by' stops at pavement cafés, triggered flashbacks to all those entrancing French films I had seen, in which actors and actresses not only sounded but looked different from us, more romantic by far than their Hollywood counterparts. And here all around was the world they had inhabited, the real thing, though now in the process of a jarring change.

What had long since happened in London, the virtual take-over of the West End by the G.I.s was happening here. American wolf-whistles greeted the chic Parisiennes, 'wafting perfume, swinging the bright tightly-rolled umbrellas that seem the fashion': American voices issued from a romantic relic of bygone days, 'a hansom cab rumbling over cobbles in a leafy square': the Olympic, now a forces' theatre, was packed with hundreds of G.I.s, 'cheering indiscriminately a revue by an all-French cast'.

"I wonder how far the American occupation will oust the terrific pro-British enthusiasm we encountered seven weeks ago," the Paris diary ends. "British correspondents I have met see it happening already – the loud-mouthed Yanks throwing their weight around, taking all the kudos. Not that they are all like that. How different I will now be finding out."

The first stretch of the four-day trip from Paris to Maastricht took us not only in the wake of the German retreat but through a countryside where a far more horrific war had been waged less than thirty years before. In the two nights we spent at Verdun, billeted in a bleak 1893 barracks where, in the American 12th Army Group's briefing room, huge maps of a new Western Front only partially concealed life-size murals of heroically posed Nazis, it was as much on that war that my thoughts were centred, and of the time I was last here.

"A German air raid a few weeks back had damaged the centre of this war-fated town. Amongst the places hit were the church and the smart hotel where, eight years ago, we had stayed during a school tour that took in the Great War battlefields, little thinking I would one day return en route to another war."

Our party of six warcos were driven the 350 miles to Maastricht in three jeeps, the comfortless vehicle I was to spend much of my time in during the next three months, hard-seated, cramped, and so flimsily enclosed that, even on these sunny October days, it became so blusteringly cold when travelling at speed (sometimes touching 60 mph) that I was more than glad of my Simpson's sheepskin coat.

Arrived at Spa in Belgium in the afternoon of the third day, Jimmy Holburn of *The Times*, my jeep companion, and I, after checking in at the Hotel Portugal, made straight for the baths. "Still blue about the lips, it was bliss to immerse ourselves in hot medicinal water. In a deep and capacious copper bath, the water came up to my neck – water that fizzed and bubbled like champagne. As I luxuriated in steam, the sky throbbed to the familiar sound of a buzz-bomb, now being rocketed to recently liberated Liège, Brussels and Antwerp – a case of sour grapes if ever there was one."

Spa, in a lap of the wooded Ardennes, was the headquarters of the American First Army, which was holding the middle sector of the line, with the American Third Army to the south, and the American Ninth to the north, and had just celebrated a notable victory, the capture of Aachen, 20 miles to the north, the first German city to fall to the Allies. At the Hotel Portugal I found that Stanley Baron, our man with the First, exhausted after a two-week coverage of a battle that had left much of the Emperor Charlemagne's capital in ruins, was taking a break in Brussels.

Cognac with beer chasers proved a rash mix that night in a lounge bar crowded with warcos, all American except for Peter Lawless of the *Daily Telegraph*, a burly, jovial man whose air of a hunting-shooting-fishing English squire went down well with the Yanks. "Towards midnight a sing-song was under way, ranging from De Old Folks at Home and Juanita to ditties that would find no place in a community song book. By two o'clock I found myself alone with an Associated Press correspondent, arguing the relative merits of Churchill and Roosevelt. When I left for bed he was leaning over the bar, holding the hands of the proprietor's daughter, praising her 'façade' and murmuring 'Ah! Madame!'

"24 October. Brutally awoken at 8.30, 9 and 9.30, I tottered down to the waiting jeep at 9.45. An appalling hangover made me almost oblivious of the 50-mile drive to the Dutch border town of Maastricht. Our billet is the Hotel Lévrier et L'Aigle Noir (Greyhound and Black Eagle), a most comfortable establishment with a massive front gateway that opens on to a wide flagged passage running the length of the hotel round a central courtyard. There is electric light, hot water, central heating. I share room 14 with Holburn.

"After a lunch I could scarcely face, I sought my bed and slept till five, and after supper went out for a moonlight exploration. The wide Meuse segregates the factory area and railway, where for the first time on the Continent I saw a train move. This side the town is spacious, tree-bedecked, in parts ancient. At the top of our street is the very wide Market Square, the 17th century Town Hall in its midst. The clock tower has a most alluring chime – a music-box tune which has magic at night. It strikes now as I write – burgomasters, Dutch interiors, skaters on a frozen lake."

Activities at the Hotel Lévrier revolved around Major Barney Oldfield, the Ninth Army's suave Public Relations Officer, from whom, eleven years after the war, I was to receive a printed postcard depicting a helmeted Donald Duck reading a hefty volume entitled 'Never a Shot in Anger', with a startled exclamation issuing from his beak – 'WAC! Barney Oldfield even mentions Michael Moynihan in this book' – and a message from Barney: "I have no objection to your use of this as a column inset, a TV closeup, or just showing it around in bars."

Challenged by that word 'even', I duly ordered a copy of the book from the New York publishers, to find that my name was mentioned, just the once, as were those of a majority of the other fifty or so warcos, who doubtless had also fallen for the bait. My name appeared in the three paragraphs devoted to the twelve British war correspondents under Barney's care, written in a way that revealed more about himself than us.

"Britain's major newspapers were strongly represented. Noel Monks, who had begun his war covering in Abyssinia, was not only a first-ranker among all the military writers, but stood that way to his paper, the *Daily Mail*. He had done much to emblazon the magnificent record of the RAF in the Battle of Britain. Jimmy Holburn fed *The Times* and roomed with Michael Moynihan of the *News Chronicle*, who later changed with Ronnie Walker. David Walker, one of the best informed on continental affairs in peace and war, had unusual competition on his own paper, the tabloid *Daily Mirror*, in the form of a pen-and-ink concoction, a cartoon-strip girl called Jane, an absolute must for British readers. Hardly a day passed that she didn't get almost all her clothes completely off. The one day she did coincided with a British advance of eight miles! There was no denying Jane was powerful stuff for a mere writer like David Walker to compete with, but he tried manfully with some success.

"The British provincial chain of the publishing giant Lord Kemsley, started us off with E.V. Kingdom and then replaced him with a journalistic jumbo, Larry Fairfield. The *Daily Express* had Laurence Wilkinson, who had hitherto covered the war from what most of the 'pros' referred to as a 'comfort station', the neutral capital of Lisbon, Portugal. The Labourite *Daily Herald* split its creditation amongst Stanley Bishop, Wing Commander Charles Bray and beauteous Iris Carpenter, a stunning blonde operating from quarters given her in various field hospitals. Peter Lawless spent part of his time with the First Army, part with us and was the *Daily Telegraph* man. That well of deep thought and sound information, the *Observer*, gave us Eric Wigham.

"The pet of the Press Corps was Alfred M. Lee of the *Huddersfield Examiner*. His home town was near the dreary moors of the Brontë sisters, but though there wasn't a British boy in the Ninth and no Huddersfield angle to write about, he chose the Ninth to ride with to Berlin and the end of the war."

From Barney's racy, anecdotal, thoroughly egocentric memoir one would hardly know that there had been a war of mounting ferocity going on out there. The picture I have of him is seated at his cluttered desk in a corner of the lobby lounge, next to the notice board and teleprinter, exchanging wisecracks with the poker school that seemed always in play at a nearby table, a dapper, slightly podgy figure, described by Iris Carpenter as 'a stand-in for Charles Boyer, with the wrong accent'. But *Never a Shot in Anger* did prove valuable in filling in the gaps in my diary, particularly concerning the domestic drama that had become the talk of Maastricht shortly before I arrived.

When Barney had picked on the Hotel Lévrier as an ideal headquarters for the press corps, he had learned that it had been commandeered by the invading German army in May, 1940, and used ever since as a German officers' billet, and that, as the townsfolk became increasingly starved of food, the sight of the Dutch proprietor, Mynheer van Egerschot, serving succulent meals and pouring wine for the hated occupiers, was something he would now find it hard to live down. Also under suspicion were his son Willem and Willem's beauteous wife Yvonne.

An example had already been made of Maastricht's most notorious woman collaborator – head shaved, she had been paraded through the streets in a cart, with her skirt hitched above her waist, while jeering crowds greeted her with cries of "Oh look! Now we see what only Germans have seen for four years!" Barney believed Mynheer van Egerschot's protestations that there had been no way he could have prevented the Germans commandeering his hotel, and that his family's patriotism was known to the Dutch underground, to whom Yvonne had passed on valuable information gleaned by Willem. But he was not altogether surprised when three plain-clothes Dutch police came to search the hotel for any incriminating evidence, possibly a secret radio on which they could now be in touch with the Germans.

Barney's account of how Willem had panicked at the sight of the police and fled to the third floor where, cornered by them, he had hurdled the guard rail at the top of the stairwell in an attempt to leap across to the second floor, only to hit the chandelier and plummet to the tiled floor below, suggests that there may have been cause for suspicion. All I recall is that the badly injured Willem was in hospital for a number of weeks and that Barney was making the most of his absence. He makes no further reference to Yvonne, and it could be that she had come into the category of the WAAF officer Barney described having met in London – 'blonde, charming, unavailable'.

My preferred jeep companions in the search for stories were Jimmy Holburn, my avuncular room-mate; Noel Monks, whom Barney had omitted to mention was an Australian, an old buddy of Alan Moorehead, whose American warco wife, Mary Walsh, had only recently jilted him for Ernest Hemingway; David Walker, a fluent linguist and so much the charming, cultivated English gentleman that the *Mirror* seemed quite the wrong stable for him; Lew Gannett, bespectacled correspondent for the *New*

York Herald Tribune, where he had been their chief book critic, the American I felt most empathy with, his addiction to poker apart.

A daily briefing was given in the spacious press room, where a huge map of Western Europe covered an entire wall, and, at the end of the day, batteries of typewriters clattered out despatches aimed at grabbing attention for a front line where, for the present, nothing much was happening.

Many years after the war, sifting through a caseful of old letters and papers, I came across a sheaf of yellowing documents, the censored copies of all the despatches I had typed at Maastricht. Most of those prior to the German breakthrough were drily factual accounts of what was happening, often requiring an arrowed map to make sense of. By contrast the spontaneously written diary entries I penned most nights communicate the excitement of not knowing what each day will bring and of being witness to historic happenings. After five years of war the fighting was at last being waged on German soil.

"25 October. After a detailed briefing we drove this morning, in a party of four jeeps, over the border into Germany. The transition was hardly noticeable – a German eagle painted on the wall of a post-office, 'strasse' instead of 'straat' on street names. Our entry was by the border town of Horzgenrath, partially industrial, with a network of battered railways. We stopped for lunch at a Divisional HQ housed in a glider factory. A colonel afterwards conducted us on a tour of the 'bulge' through the Siegfried Line, pierced in the offensive that started on 2 October.

"Driving through Kohlscheid, where Americans occupy one half of a street, Germans the other, there were occasional startling bursts of artillery fire from close at hand, but little else to suggest a war in progress. In the fields on both sides of an anti-tank ditch – first defence of the Siegfried Line – peasants worked in the fields, carting potatoes and swedes. It was in its way a reassuring sight, though these were the Enemy and the food they dug was to keep more of the Enemy alive. As they passed, leading carts along the country roads, they appeared neither more nor less than human. Five years' propaganda was shaken by close inspection of those sometimes enquiring, more often impassive faces: the mirage-country of terror and brutality, conjured over a long period by cinema, press and radio, must inevitably dissolve . . .

"26 October. A 200-mile jeep-journey in bitter weather. Our objective – Noel Monks, Lucas, the Brazilian correspondent, and I – was the U.S. 105th Division, part of the Ninth Army but now on loan to the British. North of Antwerp we found them encamped in a pine forest and under intermittent shellfire. The Americans now in the line were new to battle and having a tough initiation. After a tepid lunch in an icily draughty tent we met General Terry Allen, an experienced campaigner, small, wizened, affable, who took us to his caravan to show us how the battle was going.

"We returned via Brussels – noisy, bustling, vulgar and very much alive. It has the reputation of being the gayest of the liberated cities, even outdoing Paris. No city celebrated its liberation for so long and so ardently. It is the first place where I have had a tip refused: a waiter in a café gave me back a ten-franc note and picked two coins from the table.

"A cold two hours back. At dusk the countryside came more intimately alive. Canals and streams ran coldly bright through the fields, poplars shivered against a pale streak of sky. A level-crossing brought us to a halt beside a small roadside chapel adjoining a cemetery. The door was open, light streamed out from candles on the altar, before which knelt a young priest. From a house opposite a woman came with the keys to lock up when he had done praying. Her presence at the doorway must have been felt by him for he rose immediately. They stood talking and smiling in the little patch of light on the grass; then he got on his bicycle and pedalled away.

"Incidents no more eventful than that, glimpses of warm cottage rooms, through curved massive doorways of a muddy yard piled with straw and trodden by cattle, hint at a continuity of existence that makes even war of only passing significance. I thought of Thomas Hardy's 'Only a man harrowing clods' poem written in the Great War – 'Yet this will go onward the same/ Though Dynasties pass'.

"27 October. We were invited to 2nd Armoured Division HQ to meet General Harmon ('Old Gravel Voice'), the man who had driven his tanks with such lightning speed from Normandy to the Siegfried Line, now tipped to be first at the Rhine. A table loaded with Scotch and Martinis preceded him and drink and talk flowed smoothly. At lunch I was seated next to the Commanding Officer of the infantry, who are now having a monotonous time in the static line of the 'bulge'. Every five days they are allowed the freedom of Heerlen, but told before leaving, 'We expect you to get somewhat drunk and have a woman, but see that no one gets into trouble.' The policy has worked. A doughboy was recently found walking round and round a block in the early hours – he had been circling for over an hour, trying to sober up.

"Noel Monks and I drove afterwards into Germany. Our jeep driver, who knew the roads well, took us out to the furthest point of penetration. It was at the end of a little road in the outskirts of the village of Baesweiler. The village was dead and deserted except for a few doughboys patrolling its streets rather aimlessly. They appeared glad to see visitors for they saluted or waved. Most of the inhabitants had cleared out or were living underground in the coalmine near the village – which is still being worked.

"The little road was flanked by two-storey modern villas, now badly knocked about. Curtains flapped through broken glass; stairways were blocked with débris; the trim little front gardens were littered with splintered branches, the bright blooms of chrysanthemums were crushed and uncared for. In a back garden a soldier was tipping refuse from a pail and a lonely chicken scuttled into the undergrowth.

"At the end of the road, where it runs into the Aachen–Gladbach highway, you have come as far as you can into Germany. Three Sherman tanks, two in the gardens of the end houses, one in an allotment, form the static spearhead of the journey to the Rhine. They were so well camouflaged that I was startled on looking up to see the faces of two soldiers watching us from the open hatch.

107

The tank was all but hidden under a canopy of branches and copper-coloured leaves. We asked what was doing. 'Nothing,' said one. 'Quiet all day. A bit of shelling in the night.'

"We walked out on to the highway and looked north to the village of Setterich, some 800 yards away. A church steeple rose from a wood, hazy silhouettes in the October mist. The Germans were there, returning our gaze across a No-Man's-Land of fields. They had evidently the advantage of an observation post and field-glasses, for scarcely had we turned back into the cover of the villas when a sound as of an escape of steam rushed towards us. The shell whined overhead and landed some 500 yards beyond. It was a gesture, at any rate, an admonition to overweening curiosity.

"28 October. Some of us this afternoon went to an art exhibition in the bowels of a mountain. We were conducted by a Herr Van Poppel, Director of the Depository of Pictures and Art Treasures. A narrow cul-de-sac in the hill country outside Maastricht brought our jeeps to a halt in front of an arched gateway cut into the rock. A notice described the place as an Historic Monument. It is literally that – treasures more precious than Ali Baba's entombed beneath solid rock.

"With Herr Director as guide, we required no 'open Sesame'. He led us down a well-lit tunnel, entrance to a vast honeycomb of subterranean passages. From Roman times these hills have been quarried for limestone: before the war they were a favourite expedition for tourists; during the war they have provided an air raid shelter for 70,000 and an escape route for Allied airmen shot down. The tunnel brought us to the offices of the Director and his staff of armed guards – well-furnished rooms, with electric light, heating, prints of Old Masters on the walls, a radio playing Mozart.

"We signed the visitors' book, were asked to 'give up your weapons, please', and ushered to where a massive yellow-painted steel door had swung back. The treasure-chamber was dimly lit and crowded with its priceless collection. Eight hundred paintings, nearly half of Holland's art collections, are stored here, in addition to tapestries, drawings, old documents. Most of the paintings are hung on sliding steel frames – a notable exception being Rembrandt's Night Watch, which has been wound round a wooden roller and housed in what looks like a dog kennel.

"We went in slow contemplation down the lines of steel screens. As they slid back the guide holding the arc-lamp illuminated first one, then another of the Old Masters – and a few 'moderns'. Rembrandt, Franz Hals, Vermeer, Jan Steen, Pieter de Hooch, Ruisdael, Van der Weyden, Rubens, Van Dyck, Aieronymus Bosch, El Greco, Tintoretto, Van Gogh – these were the names spoken by the Director.

"Hidden from the light of day, a dead Holland came resplendently to life: peasants and gallants in evening revelries on the green: boisterous company in the tavern: fairs and markets: skaters on a dark frozen lake: pancakes in the kitchen: the quack in the bedroom: Burgomasters in full regalia: old women placid in almshouses: ladies, lace-capped, long-nosed: young noblemen with sensuous mouths and acquisitive eyes. Two hundred, three hundred years have not faded the lustre of robes and sparkle of eyes. But never can the gay, solemn, bawdy, gentile company have been confined into such a close prison.

"We learned that the pictures had first been buried in sand dunes, removed here in 1942 for protection from Allied bombing. They were brought by special train and the Germans could not be kept in ignorance of the hide-out. In fact a number of officers had been to see them – there had been no attempt at looting. The remainder of the Dutch collection are housed in a concrete building near the Friesland village of Steenwijk, still in German hands.

"29 October. Jimmy Holburn, Lew Gannett and I toured round to get a picture of how the German civilian is being treated. A Maastricht paper yesterday came out with a statement that 'the Americans are behaving exactly as the army of Our Lord once acted: 'There is more joy in heaven over one sinner that repenteth than over 100 righteous men'. There seems to be more joy over one German who abjures Hitler than over 100 Dutchmen who never want to have anything to do with him."

"We found little justification for this charge except that the Germans evacuated to Holland have been fed on army rations; that, by Dutch standards, is luxury. In Germany they must fend for themselves; work parties in the fields are under armed surveillance, others at fixed periods may not leave home or shelter, restrictions include a ban on patriotic music. Although furtive liaisons between women and soldiers undoubtedly occur, no 'criminal acts' against Americans have been reported. An officer described the civilian reaction as 'docile or cowered submission'.

"At Horzogenfath we called on the German burgomaster, one of 15 'puppet mayors' in the area. In a small well-appointed office I listened without comprehension to a long harangue – the other two knew German – which rose to a crescendo at one point with a pounding of the table. That was when he referred to the 'communist' element in the neighbourhood – 'communism' masquerading as Naziism being the root cause of Germany's troubles. He had two things to ask us: couldn't more work parties be allowed in the fields, and couldn't the Americans be deterred from removing furniture from houses and selling it to the Dutch for cognac?

"2 November. After two uneventful days, Noel Monks, David Walker and I drove to Brussels for a night out. After a few pre-lunch Martinis at a select bar, we fed at the correspondents' hotel, the Canterbury, where I met Jimmy Wellard, *Daily Express*, whose place on the *Chronicle* I took almost exactly two years ago. An afternoon's shopping dazed us with the abundance of goods for sale. I contented myself with a fountain pen, pipe, tobacco pouch and a bottle of cognac. A news-vendor refused to take money for an evening paper. In a vast crowded café a Belgian lady insisted on paying for my beer and was hurt I did not go with her to see a famous Brussels' square.

"I rejoined the others and a round of luxurious clubs – open to Allied officers – ensued. The bands were good, drinks abundant, women no less chic than Parisiennes. About 8 p.m. three rings on a doorbell gained us admittance to an upstairs restaurant, very comfortable and 'select'. At the bar we encountered Wing Commander Kilmartin, one of the original fighter-aces, and King Leopold's attaché. The dinner which, with a bottle of Chianti, cost us 500 francs each, was memorable, its climax the arrival of a whole roast chicken for approval (we approved). The police must have turned a blind eye on this restaurant, it being a resort of correspondents. From here on to 'The Abbey' and 'Nellie's' before 10.30 curfew.

"4 November. A night at Spa to see Stan Baron, back on his beat. After lunch we walked through the bright autumn woods of the Ardennes, quenching thirst from a tumbling stream. Further afield there is still boar-hunting and (more recently) the hunting of Germans in a pine forest. Drink and dinner and office scandal at the Portugal . . .

"11 November. This week has been mostly inactive, days merging in a time-marking round of sleeping, eating, briefing, reading, grimacing at Maastricht beer, a bitter dark liquid innocent of alcohol. Maastricht night life is confined to American films in the town theatre – once a Jesuit church – and a few crowded cafés loud with jazz. The alternatives are chess, poker and reading. Lew Gannett is intrigued by my current escapist choice – Guedella's Life of Wellington, my school prize copy of Adrian Bell's Suffolk trilogy (reminding me how I, too, wanted to be a farmer) and the Travels of Marco Polo.

"We have been invaded by a party from SHAEF – mainly American women correspondents – and on Monday were invited to dinner by the Town Major at his elegant, German-furnished headquarters. The burgomaster and his wife were guests of honour. Blackberry brandy, rum and white wine enlivened the proceedings. A friend of Gerald Fisher's, also a conducting officer, David Beavis, sat by me at dinner (he has brought a British party of three) and we conducted a correspondence down the long table with one of the women correspondents on the subject of her hat; she wore it throughout the meal, a hat like a bus conductress's. The notes mystified her and she came for an explanation. We discovered that she was a daughter of Thomas Mann, Erika; she further stated that I reminded her of her husband, W.H. Auden, having only married to wangle a passport for herself. I can only imagine she did not take a good look at him.

"Maastricht, apart from its social limitations, is a pleasant town. Behind the spacious Cathedral square there are old Dutch houses in quiet backwaters. In the gloom of the Cathedral

111

the air is heavy with incense, old men and women strike attitudes as they kneel or finger their beads; in the cloisters girls from a convent school turn to stare as they chant responses to a nun's mumblings.

"Down by the tree-lined canal parallel to the wide Meuse with its fallen bridge, stands the 13th century Helpoot, oldest city gate in Holland. It is extraordinarily well preserved and admirably set off by moat, lawns and trees. Imagination can extend the massive walls and ramparts round a medieval city and people turrets and slit windows with defiant faces. Nowadays they construct pill-boxes, anti-tank ditches, concrete dragons' teeth, and call it the Siegfried Line.

"15 November. Beer, a buffet supper and American nurses at an Evacuation Hospital outside Maastricht. It was once a Jesuit reformatory, more recently a Hitler Youth school. The party was dull but afterwards David Beavis, Eric Wigham and I followed an affable surgeon to his room and a bottle of whisky. He was Scotch-American, father an Edinburgh minister, a good talker, and took us on deer hunts and to the ski slopes of his New Hampshire mountains.

"Afterwards he took us round the wards and laughter suddenly froze at sight of a young handsome American with both legs cut short at the knee. One of the prettier nurses leaned forward from the bed beside him, talking in a low tender voice. In another bed a negro lay with closed eyes, lips drawn back from his teeth. It seemed indecent to stand and stare at these men . . .

"16 November. At 12.45 today the Big Attack was launched. We watched the ceremony from the front-line village of Beggendorf; the thunder of artillery and aircraft, the roar and splutter of tanks, the steady tramp of boots in mud, was the music of action. Thank God the waiting is over and there is something to do and write about."

CHAPTER ELEVEN

From hindsight the long-awaited Allied offensive was a mere flash in the pan in the light of the pending German breakthrough. At the time, after a 'Top Secret' briefing by General William Simpson, the Ninth Army's Commanding Officer, it seemed almost to equate with that beginning of the end in Normandy. Bolstering this optimism were the visits to Maastricht, before and during the offensive, of Field-Marshal Montgomery, shortly to take the American First and Ninth Armies under his wing. We were not to know that he had found 'no grounds for optimism' in what he had seen and heard in the American sector, and that his verdict on 'Big Simp', the U.S. Army's only totally bald general, was "a delightful man and extremely easy to work with, but not really very much good as an Army Commander".

The regular entries in my diary give a very different picture from the few impersonal despatches that were used, a close-up view of front-line fighting that reinforces my Normandy impression of it as "a squalid and casual business".

"16 November. From 2nd Armoured Divisional Command Post – in a battered farmhouse – we gazed at a sky filled with aircraft, thunderbolts with blazing canon, bombers drumming in formation high overhead, invisible fighters scrawling vapour-signatures in space. Flak burst above the enemy positions and aerial rockets cascaded in trails of white smoke. The tanks began to emerge from the farm-yards and barns and trundled over the open country to disappear over the skyline.

"We drove on to Beggendorf, a long muddy street with hardly a house habitable. The Company C.P. was in the cellar of one of these houses. Groping down through darkness we found a Captain busy with telephones in the dim light of oil lanterns. "Hello, Sapphire, Hello, Sapphire. Are you all right?

Getting hot? Take cover, get your head down. Hello, Yellow, what can you see?" The voices we could not hear came from infantry platoons advancing with trailing communication wire into battle. Before long they were reporting American tanks in the first village, Loverick, and Germans scrambling with white flags from their foxholes.

"A mortar shell exploded across the street above us. There was a tinkling of glass and dust showered from the ceiling. A soldier stumbled down the dark cellar steps and stood breathless in the lamplight. Our driver followed hot on his heels as another explosion shook the ceiling. 'Hope the jeep's still there,' said the driver. 'Moynihan?' queried the captain in a pause of telephone conversation. 'That's a good old Jewish name.'

"With reports that the first batch of prisoners were approaching the village we emerged into daylight as seven dishevelled Germans entered the farmyard at the back of the house. One was wounded; blood dripped from a trouser leg. He was motioned to a sofa that stood incongruously in a corner of the yard; one of his companions attended to the wound. Scarcely had the seven been searched and relieved of lethal weapons (a pair of nail-scissors tinkled among the mound of revolvers and cartridges) than some forty more slouched into the yard, the American guards shouting at them like drovers. One burly youth who had tried to pull a gun was pushed roughly from the ranks and made to sit cross-legged on the ground against a motor-bike, hands behind his head.

"The shouting Yanks were silent when a jeep drove slowly under the archway. An American sprawled on the back seat. Six soldiers lifted him carefully on to a stretcher, his bleeding hand having been disengaged from the butt of a machine gun. Blood covered his face and hair; he was unconscious. They carried him indoors and the prisoners watched with mild curiosity. 'Here's another,' someone shouted. There was no visible injury; the dead whiteness of his face was worse than blood. But he was alive, a leg twitched, and they carried him indoors.

"A photographer was busy among the prisoners and wounded. It was the usual sordid backwater of war. Death is cheap. The bullet missed me and you – he was hit. If he lives it will

114

be hereafter a maimed life. Later it will be important, not now. 'Get them out of here! Get the bastards moving!' The bedraggled cavalcade moves out into the road and the shooting dies away. 'Come and see us any time,' says the captain. 'We'll be around.' Another mortar explodes. We climb into our jeep and the wind rushes at our faces.

"18 November. It was the usual scene – the silent sullen prisoners in their dirty green uniforms, alert menacing Americans shouting if arms were lowered or a word spoken. A dead German lay unnoticed, his face already frozen into a waxwork grimace, until an American motioned one of the Germans to cover the body. The man ripped a muslin curtain from the window and pegged it over the body with bricks.

"An officer of the Department of Psychological Warfare sought a candidate among the prisoners for a surrender appeal to those who still resisted. The prisoners turned to the only officer among them, a young Nazi who had incurred the wrath of his captors by saying, 'I was at Smolensk. The Russians are tough fighters, not like you Americans!' His thin lips tightened at the suggestion that he might broadcast to his comrades to lay down their arms and save useless bloodshed.

"21 November. Everywhere in this countryside is evidence of German community digging – foxholes, fire trenches, L-shaped dugouts, anti-tank ditches. Some of the dugouts are cosy retreats, roofed over, with drain-pipe chimneys, well furnished inside. Near the front you never know what lurks inside. Ramage, the only British photographer, a perky Cockney, dived into one dugout when a shell landed uncomfortably close. In the darkness he heard a voice: 'Don't shoot! Don't shoot me!' Imagining it to come from a fellow-shelterer, play-acting, he groped forward until he felt the man, saying, 'Of course I wouldn't do that, sweetheart!' There was no reply. His hands outlining the man came rigidly to halt on contact with a German helmet. Ramage broke surface with alacrity and within a matter of minutes a German officer was being led away by two G.I.s. 'And I didn't even get his binoculars,' was Ramage's lament.

"22 November. In Loverick this morning Noel Monks and I were cross-examining a batch of Panzer prisoners in the porch of the caved-in church when guns opened up on all sides with shattering suddenness. 'Jerry planes!' someone cried. It was indeed the Luftwaffe making its first daylight appearance on the front. Six ME 109s, on a hurried strafing expedition, flashed into sight, flying low. Anti-aircraft gunners, starved of action for so long, greeted them in no uncertain fashion. The sky was dizzy with red tracer bullets; close beside us a machine gun blazed away with the jerky stuttering of a policeman's rattle. The reception was too hot for the German fighters, who disappeared speedily through low cloud. The young Nazi who had just been telling us that the war would soon be over was torn between pride and incredulity.

"22 November. In the shell-torn, mud-caked village of Langsweiler, fifteen civilians were found this morning in a cellar. We were taken to see them and David Walker, a foreign correspondent in Berlin before the war, got going on a farmer and his family. For six weeks they had been hiding in the cellar in fear of their lives. Where propaganda and persuasion had failed, S.S. troops have been using force to evacuate inhabitants of this area, even breaking down doors and throwing hand grenades into cellars.

"Cooking was by night to avoid detection and the farmer's son would creep above-stairs in the small hours to fetch water and supplies. The sounds of war rolled nearer until two days ago it broke shatteringly overhead, with house-to-house fighting. 'For ten years Hitler has deceived us,' the farmer's wife said bitterly. 'We do not wish any more the name of 'German'.' How often, we wondered, would *that* be said in the weeks to come.

"25 November. The front being more or less static, Alf Lee of the *Huddersfield Examiner* and I decided on a flight in a Piper Cub and made for the Artillery Group C.P. at Siersdorf. The C.O., a Colonel Hinton, said we were the only correspondents to have visited the outfit since their landing in France on D+12, and received us with great affability, celebrating the occasion with Scotch before lunch in a windowless, doorless farmhouse kitchen.

"At the air-strip I donned a parachute and clambered into the narrow space behind Lt Clarence Kingham of Ponca City,

Oklahoma. The little machine bounded forward and slowly climbed to 800 feet. We were one of some fifteen Cubs circling and hovering impudently over the battle-line, like hawks in the sunlight hovering for victims. German artillery, knowing they are out to locate enemy batteries and radio back their positions, show a healthy respect for the cocky little machines, though they are sometimes subjected to small-arms fire.

"Our fighter-bombers had been active this morning and the German positions were marked by the smoke of their fires. I was chiefly interested in the countryside immediately below us, across which the fighting had slowly advanced. Every ten yards was shell-cratered, every village and cluster of farm buildings had been pounded by bombs and guns. The elaborate German entrenchments overrun by the Americans assumed a lunatic sort of pattern; humped foxholes and L-shaped dugouts were carved everywhere into the fields, an anti-tank ditch, some 30 feet wide by 15 deep, was uncompleted and now waterlogged.

"South of Julich billows of black smoke poured from a factory, betokening oil. There was smoke to north, east and south, but not a sign of soldiers in the German-held fields just ahead. One puff of smoke on the furthest horizon particularly intrigued me. 'That's probably Cologne,' said Lt Kingham.

"Back with Colonel Hinton we drank cognac from the bottle to fortify us for the long, cold, dark ride home. It was my thirteenth time in the air, and tenth 'operational' flight.

"27 November. We reached Bourheim by following the path American tanks and infantry had taken two days before. Leaving our jeep at the railway we veered off into fields leading up to the village, stepping in tank tracks for fear of mines. These were the fields up which the infantry had advanced. Invisible to them on the ridge the Germans waited in trenches and machine-gun pits. The Americans as they breasted the rising had come under withering fire; six of them still lay as they had fallen, in attitudes of running.

"We skirted an allotment and clambered over a thorn hedge into the churchyard, furtively as boys might enter an orchard. But Death was the tenant here, the whining of shells announced his approach. Last week's services were posted in the porch. At about this time confessions should have been in progress. But the curtains of the confessional boxes had been blown aside by blast and they were empty. A noise of scuttling was heard. Three tame black rabbits were loping about in the central aisle, twitching their noses at the bright fragments of a saintly image.

"The churchyard path led out to the village. Our troops had taken possession last night and with them moved in the German shells. Between 6 and 7 this morning more than 800 artillery and mortar shells had descended on the village. They came over intermittently and haphazardly all the time we were there and our progress through the rubble-strewn streets was interrupted by quick dashes for the shelter of an archway or door; where shelter was not at hand we hunched our shoulders ridiculously as though to ward off a blow.

"In one farmyard scores of hutches had been blasted open and numerous black and white rabbits were loping abroad over the ruins of the village. The incongruity of their inquisitive snufflings in this place of death curiously held the imagination. It was the final touch of nightmare.

"4 December. (From a despatch, unused.) The greater part of Linnich is now ours, and it is the Ninth Army's most important capture to date. All the characteristics of the German front-line town are here. First there is the breakneck approach down the long straight road which the Germans, if they feel like it, can pepper with shells. On the two-mile stretch from Gereonsweiler to Linnich five jeeps and three trucks lie smashed in the ditches. The torn and splintered trees gruesomely frame our approach.

"Once inside progress become synchronized to the approaching whine of shells. In one street today I saw a shell land smack against the wall of a house opposite and slide towards us, only to come harmlessly to a halt. Linnich has been beaten up more than any other town in this sector. In one house a framed panorama of the town showing it as it had recently been showed its church spire, school and hospital rising above an orderly pattern of rooftops. A ghostly elegance was still discernible in the shattered streets. The ten thousand or so inhabitants had lived more prosperously than their fellow countrymen to the west. Only fifteen had been found still in residence by the Americans. There is little for the others to return to.

"The American major who was acting as our guide took us up to an attic observation post in the town hall roof. And from there I scrutinized for the first time German soldiers who were not dead, wounded or prisoners of war. Groups of two or three could be observed through binoculars walking unhurriedly over the fields, some disappearing behind a haystack, others into pillboxes. They were not left unmolested for long. The spotter beside me took a bearing, his readings were communicated to Artillery HQ, and soon, watching closely, we saw the shells land, some fifty yards wide of the mark. A new reading was given but again the shells landed short. 'We'll have to get a battery concentration later,' said the spotter apologetically.

"No town vacated by the Wehrmacht would be complete without evidence of looting. In the cellars of a large house we were shown what the Germans had been forced to leave behind. The floors were piled four feet deep with an accumulation of loot from Belgium and Holland. Linen, fine material for suits and dresses, furs, silk stockings, were mixed together with silver-ware, cutlery, tankards, cameras and a hundred and one odds and ends. Some looters had gone to the length of cutting out Dutch oil paintings from their frames, on the forlorn chance perhaps that they were priceless Rembrandts. I saw only two books. Both, unbelievably, were copies of *Gone with the Wind*.'

It was not until my return to London that I discovered how few of my despatches had been used, not even an account of the Dutch art treasures buried in a mountain. I envied Lew Gannett and the rest of the American correspondents, writing for papers with plenty of space for features as well as news. I might then have interested *News Chronicle* readers in some of the goings on at the Hotel Lévrier.

"Every device was used to make the camp a respite from the mud and cold of the front," wrote Barney in *Never a Shot in Anger*, and he had certainly set about it with a will. His first device was the hiring of a six-piece Maastricht orchestra to play at night, so that, thawed out and changed from muddy boots and clothing, we came down to dinner to the strains of a Strauss waltz or negro spiritual. To add a cabaret flavour Barney had hired a singer whom he typically describes in his memoir as "a cutie who managed to have enough low-cut gowns to make a change every night of the week". As a final touch he had a notice propped on the piano: "Anyone caught fraternizing with the singer will have his head shaved".

It was in the same vein that he describes an appearance by Marlene Dietrich, who was touring the American sector, which "ended with her playing a saw in hillbilly style – showing genuine khaki-coloured long-john underwear". What I remember was that Marlene gave us all the last known address in Berlin of her mother, Frau von Loersch, requesting that we seek her whereabouts when we got there and "no matter where you find her, get a message to me". This poignant plea was somewhat spoilt when it transpired that she had last seen her mother some time before the war and had made no contact with her since.

Barney's worthiest idea, paid for from our warcos' kitty, was a Christmas party for Maastricht children. It was staged, two days after my visit to Linnich, on St Nicholas Day, the day when the patron saint of children, attended by the dwarfish Black Pete, visits Dutch children to find out how they have behaved during the year and to dispense presents accordingly.

Tables in the dining-room had been arranged in a semi-circle, with places for 84 children aged from 3 to 12 from a Maastricht orphanage. Watching them at the candle-lit tables, eyes sparkling as they gorged sandwiches and cakes and jellies, and later went, one by one, to receive Black Pete's judgement and St Nicholas's reward, was a vision to look back on in the coming weeks.

Snow was falling and the offensive was fizzling out when five days later I left for Spa to cover for Stanley Baron, who had claimed sick leave and was unlikely to return until after Christmas. I was glad that David Walker had also been switched there and next day accompanied him on an hour-long jeep ride to the First Army front line, a front that no one could have guessed was about to become headline news.

"We drove through the snow-clad Ardennes, vast fir forests stretching dark against the snow that sparkled in the sun. Apart from this breathtaking beauty the front was much like our

120

own, with infantry and artillery slogging at pill-boxes in forest clearings, bitterly cold. We lunched at a divisional command post at Wirzfeld three miles from the front, where David met a friend from his Lisbon days, now an artillery officer. A First Army offensive was on, with the Roer dams, impregnable to four RAF attacks, as the major objective. Driving back through Christmas card country, the snow slopes tinged pink in the declining rays of the sun, it all seemed unreal. Back at the Portugal we had partridge and wine for dinner, and after drank cognac with the First Army boys.'

This minor First Army offensive apart, there was an 'All Quiet on the Western Front' feeling in the air, so much so that Monty was alerting Eisenhower that he wanted to go to England on 23 December to spend Christmas with his son, and at the same time assuring his troops that the enemy had received such a battering and was in such a bad way that "his situation is such that he cannot stage a major offensive operation".

The *News Chronicle* had evidently come to the same conclusion, for, on 15 December (the day before the breakthrough) I set off, at the editor's request, to join a large party of SHAEF correspondents being flown from Paris for a three-day tour of the American Ninth Air Force, my only companion an American photographer for the Associated Press, Pete Carrol. The diary description of a trip, that produced not a line of copy, was written retrospectively four days later.

"There was first a three-hour jeep ride through the Ardennes to Luxembourg – hills deeply crusted with snow, hairpin bends swept by a bitter wind, tidy but bleak towns like St Vith and Echternach, now front-page news, pierced by the arrows of Fleet Street map-makers. We stopped for lunch at a roadside inn miles from anywhere. A dozen or so doughboys lounged in the bar; one at a ramshackle piano was strumming through a book of American 'hit' tunes; two played cards in an abstracted way; one wrote home. The warm air, which temporarily thawed us, was heavy with ennui. No one could have guessed how soon that boredom would vanish before the thunder of Tiger tanks.

"Luxembourg is an elegant city, perched on a plateau, but there was no time to explore its ancient quarters or more recent night clubs. In the evening, having joined up with the SHAEF party, we had conferences with General Omar Bradley, Monty's opposite number, who met us individually and affably, and the Ninth Air Force commander. Dinner and drinks awaited at our hotel, whence next morning we left for the airfield and the flight to Nancy.

"There the programme was repeated, Generals Patton and Weyland briefed us; there were conducting officers, command cars, dinners, drinks strewn in our path. The whole thing was ludicrous, but the Ninth Air Force certainly went all out to get itself boosted in print. Pete Carrol and I, fresh from the First Army front, felt absurdly veteran among this busy excitable throng, elegantly attired, without mud on their boots. The whole charade made me more than ever glad that I had disobeyed orders in Normandy and made for Paris rather than this publicity-hungry outfit.

"It was, however, an enjoyable waste of time. General 'Blood-and-Guts' Patton, burly, white-haired, with an incongruously high-pitched voice and a strange way of pursing his lips and spluttering over a word, is indeed a dynamic personality; I would hate to incur his wrath. He ended his speech: 'Anything I said that is blasphemous or obscene is off the record!' From this briefing Carrol and I drove to General Weyland's house, arriving before the main party.

"It had been an architect's house and was sumptuously furnished. In the spacious thick-carpeted lounge, steps led down in one corner to a cocktail bar, and above it a ship's ladder climbed to a curtained alcove. On the opposite side of the room water gurgled in a goldfish pond let down into the floor. The bathroom was a luxurious affair in green, the General's bedroom regal. Over a chair was draped an Alsace peasant costume he had bought for his daughter, all velvet and lace.

"There was a prodigal choice of drinks and, with the arrival of the others, a lively party ensued, with Weyland, youthful, handsome and hearty, an excellent host. Towards the end of the evening we reclined on sofas and cushions on the floor to watch a collection of combat films. Across the white walls of the lounge Thunderbolts dive-bombed roads and railways, smoke and flame belched from vehicles and coaches, enemy fighters raced towards us spitting cannon fire, only to disintegrate. It was a violent transition from the lamp-lit luxury of our surroundings, but we had drunk enough only to cheer and shout 'Got him!'

"On Sunday we flew north to Vervières, where General Quesada, beaming happily, confirmed what General Patton had hinted at. The Germans were attacking, not locally, not for limited gains, but in strength and with all their might. This, said the General, might be the long awaited chance of destroying finally and irrevocably the German army in the West.

"Carrol and I left the party with all speed and returned to Spa. David Walker was typing furiously in his room in the Portugal. I had imagined at most desperate fighting four or five miles inside our lines. But Panzers were running wild deep into Belgium. Paratroops were shooting up convoys far behind the front; prisoners were talking of Liège, even Antwerp by Christmas. On a return trip to Wirzfeld, David had just in time escaped the initial stages of the breakthrough when ghostly figures had been seen advancing through the forest, white-clad, bucket-helmeted Germans camouflaged against the snow, marching abreast and followed by 60-ton Tiger tanks. The evening conference was crowded and excited; it was apparent that we could write only in general terms, and that the word 'critical' was taboo.

"Next morning the momentum of excitement gathered pace. Paratroops were reported four miles from Spa. Correspondents returned after vain attempts to reach a front now as fluid as Niagara; from Monschau and Malmédy hospitals were being evacuated. Command Posts were in chaos for the enemy were left, right and centre, fighting as they had not fought since the days of Blitzkrieg. By lunchtime we were being alerted to be ready to leave before dark.

"David and I came down with our cases and typewriters mid-afternoon to find Madame of the Portugal serving farewell drinks to correspondents as they left for waiting jeeps. 'It is the last flicker of their flame,' she said bravely, but her lip trembled. She was notoriously pro-Allied.

"The two-hour ride to Maastricht was one I shall not forget. In villages and towns Belgians lined the streets in silence as the endless convoys moved slowly in retreat. A small boy asked, in French, 'The American army is a great army? They will beat the Germans?' 'It is a great army,' David assured him. In Vervières two painted girls laughed hysterically as we passed, ousting us with vehement gesticulations. They were the only friends of the Germans we encountered. For others panic, possibly death, was round the corner.

"At Maastricht our news came as a bombshell. First Army correspondents who followed us told of Messerschmitts strafing the convoy shortly after we had passed through. During the evening we glued our ears to every vague news broadcast and discussed the incredible possibility of being surrounded. Outside guns were blazing at German raiders. The world was topsy-turvy.'

With the exception of Pearl Harbor, never had American troops been thrown into such confusion by an attack than that mounted by the Germans in the early hours of Saturday, 16 December, when artillery opened fire along an 85-mile stretch of thinly held American line to launch what became known as the Battle of the Bulge. One of the mysteries of the war is how the Allies had been totally unaware that a German offensive was brewing, and that, from early December 250,000 German troops, backed by 970 tanks and 900 guns, had been assembling behind their lines under the command of Field-Marshal von Rundstedt.

"No one knows quite what will happen next,' I wrote on 18 December, in the comparative safety of my hotel room in Maastricht. 'First Army correspondents who have fled here from Spa say that German tanks and infantry are coming down from the hills towards the town. Most of the First Army press camp has evacuated to Lìege. As I write, every ack-ack gun in Maastricht is blazing away at German planes, lighting the darkness with a fury of red tracers. Perhaps, for the third night running, they are dropping paratroops, young Nazi fanatics who have been opening up at jeeps and lorries far behind the lines. There is no longer security even as far back as here. If it were not tremendously exciting after so many weeks of our slogging advance, there might be cause for alarm. Everywhere the atmosphere is electric with speculation. Will they come?'

Hitler's plans for an all-out offensive in the West had begun to take shape as far back as July, after the Allied breakthrough in Normandy, and a Trojan Horse plan to use disguised commandos was his particular brainwave. Codenamed Operation Greif (German for the mythical Griffin), its function was to open the way to victory by infiltrating a few hundred English-speaking commando troops, wearing American field jackets over German uniforms and riding in American jeeps, trained to cut telephone wires, turn signposts to misdirect traffic, hang red ribbons along roads to indicate they were mined, and create chaos and confusion in any way they could.

In the early stages Operation Greif proved a resounding success, with all but 8 of the 40 American jeeps involved returning safely to the German lines, having left behind the impression that many more such bands were roaming around. Additional panic had been caused when one of the captured commandos intimated that a special unit had been given the mission of assassinating Eisenhower and other top Allied commanders. So seriously was this taken that for over a week Ike was made a virtual prisoner by his security force back at his Paris headquarters.

American counter-measures employed to unmask the impostors resulted in what General Bradley described as "half a million G.I.s playing cat-and-mouse with each other," and which provided an added excitement to every jeep ride we took in search of a story. Immense traffic hold-ups led to check points where American Military Police might halt any jeep that looked suspicious to determine whether the occupants were really who they said they were.

Knowledge of the password for the day was essential, but for us Brits a near-impossible test came in the American-based general knowledge quiz that followed. On the few occasions we were interrogated I recall having no idea what was the name of Betty Grable's husband (Harry James), the name of President Roosevelt's dog (Fala), the meaning of 'Dem Bums' (Brooklyn Dodgers) or even the capital of Illinois, but we were let off on the score of our very unAmerican accents and the testimony of our American drivers. Many hundred genuine G.I.s who failed a test, we learned, were hauled in for more thorough investigation. Eighteen disguised German commandos, including the one who had planted the assassination rumour, were shot as spies after capture.

"Sheer hysteria characterized many of the first press offerings from the Bulge," Barney Oldfield reveals in his memoir, and goes on to praise Captain Ed Lavelle, chief press censor for both the Ninth and First Armies, for "telling his staff to be generous with the blue pencil".

Back in Fleet Street it was less the censor's blue pencil than that wielded in News Rooms that counted, as I discovered a month later when thumbing through back-numbers in the *News Chronicle* library. Tepid headlines like "Von Rundstedt Opens 'Last Throw' Drive" had announced the traumatic start to the breakthrough, and thereafter there had been precious little sense of urgency or drama in the coverage of what the reading public must have seen as little more than a temporary diversion, a basically American affair, with Monty only brought in towards the end. Of the 24 despatches I sent over a period of 32 days, only seven were used.

What had been a major preoccupation on the Home Front during this time, I discovered, had nothing to do with war. It was indicated in a leading feature written at the height of the battle, which began, "There is concern that the number of plumbers in London will be insufficient to deal with all the cases of burst pipes that have been reported," and went on to urge a radical change in the design of post-war houses, particularly as regarding plumbing and heating.

It was the coldest winter Europe had known for 54 years.

CHAPTER TWELVE

" 'Well, how about *this* for your memoirs? Glamorous, what!'

"The voice, hoarse from long suppression, comes from the fellow-correspondent muffled to the ear-tips beside me in the lurching jeep. We have been silent for the past hour and, understanding his outburst to be à propos everything in general rather than anything in particular, I do not attempt a rejoinder.

"For one thing it would have meant disturbing the elaborate swathings of the ice-encrusted scarf covering my mouth, using gloved fingers that have long since gone numb. For another it would lead to one of those slightly disturbing looks into the future – how much all our warco activities will count for once back in the peacetime hurly-burly of Fleet Street.

"Glamorous? Certainly not for our driver, a dour youth from Nebraska, whose hunched back I can dimly make out as he peers through a meagre peephole in the windscreen. Snow swirls inexhaustibly around our dimmed headlights. Fifteen miles away, up and down the ice-surfaced Ardennes roads, lies Spa and the painful reinvigoration of brandy and hot water. It does not do to look back on the tank crews we have left in that burnt-out, snow-swamped village by the fir forest, awaiting the order to strike."

The fellow-correspondent I was envisaging in this opening to a post-war sketch was Noel Monks, and it was he who first got around to writing those memoirs, *Eye Witness*, published in 1956. A man who customarily looked on the bright side of things, even seeming to bear no grudge against the unspeakable Hemingway for having stolen his wife, gentle in speech and demeanour, he was also a man of considerable bulk, and I was intrigued by his recollection of becoming so frozen after ten hours on the Ardennes roads that he had to be hauled bodily from jeep to hotel. Could it be that I had been so benumbed as not to recollect the same thing happening to me?

The Arctic weather in the Ardennes was the common enemy to everyone engaged in the Battle of the Bulge, though some of the images I retained were of a dazzling beauty. The Germans had not retaken Spa, and I was based there until Stanley Baron got back from his sick leave, when I returned to Maastricht. Most days I drove to some part of the fluctuating front, usually with Noel or David, and one of the few diary entries I found time or energy for during this period indicates the distances involved.

"From Maastricht a round trip has entailed a long and bitter jeep-ride of some 150 miles, on perilous roads, enjoying all the comforts of a mobile ice-box. We drive through the miserable rocket-blasted streets of Liège; thereafter the road is a switchback into the serene beauty of the Ardennes, which I have now seen in every conceivable atmosphere and light, from soupy fog to the immaculate brightness of early morning, in blizzard-filled darkness and the pink unearthly glow of sunset. It will be hard ever to conceive of this fairy-tale landscape as other than a setting for war."

A despatch (unused), written when the outcome of the battle was still in doubt, describes a typical foray to the front:

"There are two ways of reaching the bleak upland village of Samree astride the Laroche–St Vith highway. The first is the way the tanks took along a narrow twisting road scooped from the hillside; the other, through a maze of forest, follows the tracks of the American doughboys.

"The footsteps are fresh in the snow and the burned wrecks of tanks lie stark in the ditches. Two hours of furious fighting in the cold light of dawn have left their trail of blood and débris for the sun to find and snow, dropping from the firs, to soften. From Amonines to Dochamps and on to Samree the icy road that overhangs the valley, where there is scarcely room for two cars to pass, is flanked with burned-out German vehicles and American tanks that have been blasted or have lost their grip to crash down the steep slope.

"Jeep driving is perilous enough and it seems miraculous that any of our tanks were able to get through to give covering fire to the infantry storming the village. As one officer said, 'This kind of warfare is not in any of the textbooks.' The Divisional General, who had fought through Italy, described it as 'the worst terrain in Europe, apart from Switzerland'. Often the spearhead was brought to a halt while engineers sprinkled the glassy road with cinders and sand. Felled trees had to be removed from their path, and only by constant mortar fire during the night were the Germans prevented from laying a forest of firs across the road. 'That effectively stopped them,' said an officer, 'from running out with their little choppers and playing at George Washington.'

"From the deep snow of a ditch the legs of a German soldier protrude. A charred and shrivelled body lies by a burned-out half-track, unrecognizable as human, black in the snow like a monkey. In deeper drifts parts of frozen bodies stick out. Not until the thaw sets in will the snow give up its gruesome burden.

"From the ruined farms and cottages of Samree the homeless villagers are trudging in a pitiful cavalcade that still smiles gratitude to the liberators. In Samree the bitter smell of phosphorus hangs around the charred houses. Last night artillery blasted and phosphorus shells smoked out the Germans from their hideouts. They are now five hundred yards east of the village. A machine gun rattles, a long plume of smoke drifts in the sunlight. In the street tank crews and infantry are stamping in the snow. They are bearded and dirty and have lost all sense of time. Many have been fighting without respite for seven days and during that time have not tasted hot food. Frostbite and exhaustion have accounted for many of our casualties. In these bitter conditions a man can stand so much and no more.

"The cruellest fighting is hidden in the half-light of the forest through which the infantry advance, guided through the maze by the air bursts of our artillery. In parts of the forest, dark and forbidding like something out of a Grimms' fairy tale, the snow is dyed red with blood where German and American infantry came to grips. Dead bodies are being ploughed from six-foot snowdrifts.

"The snow slopes are turning pink in the sun. Beauty sits strangely in the frozen valleys of death."

There must have been many descriptive despatches of this kind, relished in America, that ended up on Fleet Street spikes. Those of mine that were preferred were of the starkly factual kind that could have been written up from a briefing, among them accounts of the Malmèdy massacre and of atrocities to Belgian civilians, both, it was later to transpire, committed on direct orders from Hitler to create 'a wave of terror'.

The massacre occurred on the second day of the breakthrough, when crews of an SS Panzer regiment herded 120 G.I.s who had surrendered into a field near Malmèdy, lined them up and riddled them with machine-gun fire from two tanks. Four days later I reported having seen signed confessions from S.S. prisoners in the village of Parfondray "recounting in cold terms the murder of twenty Belgian men, women and children". "The civilians were picked up in the streets," a corporal stated, "and brought into a barn where they were shot. I then received orders to burn the barn down."

But for most newspaper readers, both in Britain and America, the Battle of the Bulge would be chiefly remembered for an episode in the American Third Army sector, the heroic stand of 11,000 men of the 101st Airborne Division, known as the 'Screaming Eagles', at Bastogne, a town at the centre of a major road network. The nine days they were beleaguered there, the reaction of their commanding officer when two German officers with a white flag brought a surrender demand (his reply was the one word 'Nuts!'), and the climax when Blood-and-Guts Patton rode his tanks to the rescue, had all the ingredients of the Hollywood epic it eventually became.

Still-beleaguered Bastogne was the chief topic of conversation in Brussels, where David Walker and I spent Christmas. "We berthed at the Palace Hotel, fed at the Canterbury, and treated ourselves to a well-earned whoopee. War is a different proposition at the Canterbury, where Larry Solon, still with the British Second Army, could entertain us in his room before dinner to a dozen oysters, champagne and the company of

130

his chic Belgian blonde. 'Puss' and 'Poppa' were the mutual endearments.

"The Big Three, Alan Moorehead (*Daily Express*), Alexander Clifford (*Mail*) and Christopher Buckley (*Telegraph*), Monty's blue-eyed boys from the Desert War days, were much in evidence, Clifford shadowed by Jenny Nicholson, ex-actress daughter of Robert Graves, whose status as a WAAF appeared merely academic. Since Normandy the three have waxed fat on luxurious, expense-paid living, rarely bothering to visit front-line troops, and have a supercilious air of having seen it all before. But at Christmas lunch too much festive celebration got the better of them, as they retired one by one to vomit.

"Other cliques are subsidiary to this established constellation. The two Russians, hard-bitten colonel and innocent-faced protégé, occupy their silent corner with occasional sardonic smiles. Tom Downes of the *London Evening News*, enormous man of action, treats me to an Elizabethan quart-jug of ale, recalling our 2nd TAF days. There was a rather constrained meeting with Ronnie Walker, who later shared wine with more affability.

"On Christmas Day I was surprised when David attended Mass (an unlikely acolyte of the Whore of Babylon), leaving me to roam the crowded streets. Belgian families with a Tommy in tow were working up an appetite for their carefully garnered Christmas lunches. Hospitality was wholesale. It would have been no problem to find a family to take us in tow.

"About nine o'clock on Christmas night we descended the stairs into the rosy light of Maxim's, crowded and noisy. After drinks David took to the dance floor and returned with a girl who claimed upbringing in Bolton. When I ordered a bottle and four glasses she fetched her sister, a plump girl who desired to be called 'Tiny'. Both spoke passable English. David claimed philosophical disquisitions; Tiny showed other ambitions which increased in vehemence at the Paris-Paris. I remember we had poached eggs somewhere else, at an exorbitant 45 francs each, but do not recall what prompted Tiny to flounce off in a rage. We returned to the Palace at seven in the morning. *C'est la guerre* – reverse side to the Ardennes, this sound of revelry by night."

Less than fifty miles from Brussels, but in quite a different world, I woke three days later to the persistent roll of gunfire and a temperature a long way below freezing point.

"Even the swiftly flowing waters of the little River Ronce outside the inn where I stayed the night were frozen into ripples of corrugated ice. Although the sun is bright, visibility is marred by the icy mist that rises from forest and valley. The enemy guns are firing with unabated ferocity as S.S. troops fight with the desperation of a last-ditch stand to stem the Allied advance as it crushes down to meet the upward thrust of the American Third Army.

"Today's fighting began at one thirty this morning, when, by the light of stars and snow, they advanced to reinforce their comrades in the bitterly contested village of Bihain. The Germans defended it almost to the last man. Its streets and ruined houses are piled with their dead."

None of this despatch was used in the *News Chronicle* of 30 December, which carried a banner headline "Rundstedt is Fought to a Standstill", and a long analytical summing up of the situation by William Forrest, our man at SHAEF HQ in far-away Rheims. But, unaware of the spike that awaited it, and bolstered by a Christmas greeting from Gerald Barry, thanking me for my 'continued good work' and awarding me a bonus, I soldiered on:

"It is lovely countryside, not unlike parts of the Lake District, and our troops hate it. In the ditches as we drove along the occupants of tanks and lorries sweated and swore in efforts to regain the icy road. The cold is intense. Outside the bleak wrecks of farms and cottages soldiers encircle huge log fires, staring from the comfort of the flames at the steel-grey dusk darkening their white world. At the edge of one forest two G.I.s were heating their evening meal at a wood fire, while, six yards away, stiff legs extended to the blaze, lay the body of a German, almost literally a skeleton at the feast.

"There are hardships and hazards about this hill and valley fighting that can only be appreciated at first hand. The crags, the endless forests dipping and rising over the hills into mists, icy streams and dark swiftly flowing rivers, lonely villages of grey stone huddled around the Gothic battlements of a castle, make up a macabre setting for this bitter conflict. In happier times well-to-do holidaymakers infiltrated from the towns with their skis and sporting rifles. The snow slopes were their playground and the forests hunting grounds of the deer and wild boar.

"History will remember it as it is today, its villages overflowing with troops, streets jammed with the traffic of war, civilians trekking the roads with bundles salvaged from the wrecks of their homes. In the fields herds of cows wander disconsolately in the snow, lumber through the frozen streets or group around the doorways of ruined farms. Amid the grim paraphernalia of war they move like ghosts of another existence. Tanks barge them aside to go thundering down the roads into battle.

"In a field behind the church two hundred prisoners are lined up with hands behind their heads while Americans go down their ranks carefully searching them. In the dusk a crowd of G.I.s has congregated to watch and shout disparaging remarks. They are a miscellaneous bunch, frightened kids of sixteen, sullen grey-haired men, arrogant long-haired thugs. They look cold and hungry and dirty and glad to have escaped from it all with a whole skin. But there are others, thousands of them, still infesting the forests that darken the horizon. Their commanders have given orders to hold on at all costs. 'Further advances were made' means quite a lot in this inhospitable land.

"9 January, 1945. A few hours after the last German snipers had surrendered, a group of American medium bomber pilots drove into Houffalize. They had come to see the results of their week-long bombing of this vital hub of von Rundstedt's salient. Nothing is now left but the skeletons of buildings, the outlines of a church. As an example of precision bombing Houffalize stands as a tribute to the skill of our pilots and air crews. As a spectacle it is horrifying.

"Apart from bulldozers clearing a path through the wreckage, the town seemed completely deserted. The eerie silence was occasionally broken by the sound of mortar fire reverberating round the hills that cup the town. But under the surface of its devastated streets life was going on – civilian life.

"It was in the low-ceilinged dank crypt of the church that

we found the seventy inhabitants of Houffalize who had lived through the deluge of bombs. For ten days it had been their home, their sanctuary. They covered every inch of floor space, young children, mothers, old men and women. As they told us of their experiences their voices warmed into animation, as might the voices of people waking slowly from a nightmare.

"For ten days they had lived on small supplies of potatoes and the flesh of cows killed in the bombing. Four old women had died from shock and privation. In other parts of the town nearly two hundred fellow-villagers had been killed. But Germans had died too. 'If you had not bombed,' said a young woman, 'the Germans would still be here.' The aged white-haired priest who had been their spiritual and mental comforter throughout their ordeal was proud of his parishioners. 'There were Germans who came into our shelter, full of terror of the bombs. My people were calm as they saw the Germans cowering about them. My people were magnificent.'

"Many of the inhabitants had found refuge from the bombing in neighbouring villages. They will be returning to find nothing left of their town. Its fifteen hotels, to which tourists flocked for winter sports and the summer beauty of the hills, are impossible to locate amongst the heaps of crumbled brick and stone. But the Germans have gone.

"15 January. In a surprisingly elegant room in an imposing house on the outskirts of the drab débris-strewn village of Achouffe, I met the men who closed the gates on Von Rundstedt's dream. Other correspondents in the past three weeks have trod its carpets, glanced appraisingly at the gilt-framed portraits, tinkled a tune on the grand piano – German correspondents. They had come to cover an epic in the annals of the Third Reich – the crossing of the Meuse, the capture of Liège and Antwerp, thus cutting off the British from their supply lines and forcing them into a second Dunkirk.

"The lady of the house smiled her relief as she welcomed us and recalled all that had passed in this room. 'They had a headquarters here. Always there was feverish activity. That room was the German commander's, here the correspondents worked, very busily.' She hammered the keys of an invisible typewriter and smiled again. 'They looked angry at having to leave.'

"Into this same room where they had agonized over their despatches, three American infantrymen now filed, unshaven, weary-eyed, and a little at a loss to know why Allied war correspondents should be interested in them. This morning they had been entrenched in the snow, with two machine guns guarding a semi-demolished footbridge on the north bank of the little River Ourthe: Sgt Dean of Toccoa, Georgia, Corporal Wynn of Clewiston, Florida, and Corporal Karos of Lisle, Illinois. At 8.30 two jeeps had come into sight on the narrow snow-covered road across the bridge.

" 'We'd been expecting Germans,' said Sgt Dean, 'but these looked like Americans. I told my men to keep them covered, shouted a challenge and crossed the river by the two logs that were left of the bridge. They were Yanks all right, Third Army boys out ahead of the tanks, looking for a road.' They shook hands. The Allied pincers through the German salient were closed.

"Very few of Von Rundstedt's men remain on the wrong side – front-line officers had never expected anything in the nature of a Falaise Gap haul. But every road running east is littered with the dead and the débris of the long columns of retreat, and this afternoon, for the first time since the start of the American offensive, fighter bombers are wheeling and diving over the escape roads.

"There were fanatical attacks on the part of the Germans in a last-ditch stand before the closing of the gap. In one battered village we passed through, sixty Germans on bicycles had sighted a medium American tank, followed by infantry. The cycle column charged the tank with the hysterical cry, 'Down with the Yankee sons of bitches!' Machine-gun fire mowed them down. They lie everywhere, Von Rundstedt's defeated heroes. Their tanks, their lorries and horse-drawn carts, strew the ditches and discolour the snow. And now relentless pressure is forcing them back the way they came a month ago, with promise of victory and hopes of glory."

The presence of German war correspondents covering the battle, so casually mentioned in what proved to be my last

135

despatch from Maastricht, had come as a revelation. It had somehow never occurred to me that we would have opposite numbers, driving around on their side of the front, typing despatches just as eulogistic of their troops, just as slanted. In retrospect my time with the Ninth Army could be seen as a gradual realization of the obvious – that there were no fundamental differences between the German and Allied soldier, German and Allied warcos, German and British civilians sheltering from bomb and rocket.

Even the atrocities that were made so much of were not peculiar to the Nazis, as I discovered when it came to light that there had been immediate retaliatory action on the part of the Americans to the Malmèdy massacre. Before an attack scheduled for the following day an order was issued to infantrymen of one American brigade stating, "No S.S. troops or paratroopers will be taken prisoner but will be shot on sight". During a battle in the village of Chegnogne, a house whose cellar was being used as a first-aid post by the Germans was set on fire, causing the twenty-one wounded soldiers in it to emerge, the first carrying a Red Cross flag, only to be mown down by machine-gun fire at the doorway.

Three months with the Ninth Army had shown, as expected, that there was no such thing as a typical American, though the stereotype of the brash, macho, gum-chewing Yank was mirrored in a number of our fellow-warcos. Others equated with the likeable Yorkshireman, Alfred Lee, described by Barney as 'regional representatives working for the home-town boy', covering for papers like the *Des Moines Register-Tribune, Tampo Tribune, St Paul Dispatch, Baltimore Sun*, and spending their time until the breakthrough tracking down local boys from their region for interviews and photographs, preferably crouched in front-line foxholes, grinning from a tank turret or fraternizing with the prettier natives.

When I returned to London towards the end of January, leaving most of my baggage behind, it was on the assumption that I would be returning after a couple of weeks leave to see the war through with the Ninth. Instead the leave extended to two months, while the office made up its mind what areas of the war most called for coverage, a period summed up in a solitary diary entry:

"It has been a long, crowded, health-sapping interval, with ten days at home and most week-ends away – Oxford, Burford, Stratford, Bath, a remote cottage on the Berkshire Downs; in London lunchtime pub sessions in Fleet Street, and gay or tranquil evenings with Ben, Carola, latterly Lisa. Too much jostles the memory that might seem trivial in writing but comes to mind clearly and delightfully."

The ten days at home gave me a chance to catch up on family affairs. All but Barbara and Geoffrey had flown the roost, and I found my parents, though as rooted as ever in their Calvinist beliefs, considerably mellowed. My father was now a Governor of Birkenhead School, active in the formation of a Parents' Association, and a devotee of the public school system he had missed out on as a grammar school boy. My mother had become a close friend of Margaret Bushell, spinster sister of the headmaster, a handsome slightly intimidating woman who had spent much of her life in the ambience of boys' public schools and envied my mother not only her large family but her religious certainties.

A cello player, Miss Bushell was the first person I knew to whom music was the supreme solace, and she had earlier endeared herself to me by giving me the matchless 1926 recording of Alfred Cortot, Jacques Thibaud and Pablo Casals playing Schubert's Trio in B Flat, confessing that she could not help crying whenever she listened to Casals' playing in the slow movement.

But, despite their acceptance of many of the ways of the world, Sunday to my parents was still the Sabbath Day to be kept holy, and I felt obliged to accept my mother's request to play a once customary role at divine service in Park Grove Strict and Particular Baptist Chapel. At some stage I had taken over from Aunt Lizzie at the harmonium, making it a condition that I could choose the hymns – hymns that, whatever the words, could be sung to a passable tune.

Nothing seemed to have changed as I sat there in the bottle-green light from the frosted windows, listening to my father's

Sunday-solemn voice and the tickings of the chimeless clock, in the pews around me the familiar faces of the Elect. Gathered outside after the service, though they took it in turn to shake my hand, I was relieved that no one quoted a text at me, not even Mr Sloane, who was evidently taking a long time to get his life over with.

What confronted me when, after a summons, I returned to the office was the last thing I had expected. On one wall of the Foreign Room a large map of the world was pinned, and to this Norman Cliff smilingly steered me. "Now where would you like to go?" he asked, and waved his left hand loosely over Holland and Germany. "Back there? Or – " his right hand moved a long way east and came to a hovering halt on what looked to be the blue expanse of the Pacific Ocean – "there?" He smiled again. "The British Pacific Fleet. I don't suppose you've even heard of it!"

I hadn't. For me, as for most people in Britain, the war in the Pacific had always been a shadowy affair, largely the concern of the Americans, and few were aware that, by agreement between Churchill and Roosevelt, a British Pacific Fleet had been created to ensure an active role for Britain in the final stages of the Far Eastern War.

I asked Norman for time to think about it, but it did not take me long to decide that, having sampled the Air Force and Army, now was the chance to join the Navy and see a bit more of the world. So it was that, in due course, I received a letter from Maastricht:

"Dear Mike, Everybody here was sorta put out with the *News Chronicle* for having decided you should go to the big fish and Jap waters, but if they're paying you, I guess there's not much we can do about it. It goes without saying that everybody is genuinely sorry that you're not coming back.

"We are sending your bed-baggage-and-mail back to you by our pony express route via the office of Major Madary in Paris on the Stars and Stripes courier.

"I have asked Al Lee to give me any money he owes you and he, having been on another of the organized binges we throw around here, is not at all sure whether or not he doesn't owe you something, now that I've brought it up.

"All the best of everything, Mike, and I hope, if we have to move the Ninth Army in on Chinese soil, that you'll come in for a chow mein dinner with us and stay on.

"Regards from Griff and all the boys,

"Yours, Barney!"

Unrecorded, though hinted at in my diary entry, were the highlights of this protracted leave, my meetings with Lisa. Our usual rendezvous, when not with Ben and Carola, was the Café Royal in Regent's Street, than which I could not have imagined anywhere more redolent of romance.

A pre-war *Picture Post* feature I had kept had described the Café Royal as "the nearest approach in London to the restaurants of Paris and Vienna, the meeting-place of cosmopolitans and Bohemians, and one of the most famous rendezvous in the world," tracing its history from the Naughty Nineties (Oscar Wilde, Aubrey Beardsley, Frank Harris, W.B. Yeats) through Edwardian times (Walter Sickert, William Orpen, Whistler, Augustus John, Somerset Maugham) to 1938 ('candid camera' shots of Jacob Epstein, Constant Lambert, Alexander Korda, Charles Laughton, seated at the crowded café's famous marble-topped tables).

Wartime had given an added savour to this Bohemian atmosphere – the red-plush seats and gilded mirrors, the white-aproned waiters, the hubbub of voices and laughter, the spirals of tobacco smoke drifting to the painted ceiling – and we established an easy intimacy as we got to know each other.

Lisa, I learned, had lost her adored father when she was seven, and had never been close to her mother and elder sister. Of her varied war work the most interesting was the only one she did not want to talk about. For fourteen months, from October, 1941, she and Carola had worked together, under vows of secrecy, for MI5, travelling daily from Oxford to their work-place, a Nissen hut in the grounds of Blenheim Palace. Not until after the war did she divulge that their job had been to vet candidates for the ENSA shows that toured the battlefronts, but had themselves become suspects through Carola's friendship with a known Communist and asked to leave.

Now working at an Experimental Aircraft Factory, Lisa travelled from Slough for our meetings until the evening when a special arrangement had been made. Helen, a novelist friend of hers, had given her the keys to her Notting Hill flat and we took a taxi to it from the Café Royal. When subsequently I saw that Edwardian semi-detached in broad daylight, it looked ridiculously ordinary, unrelated to the magic of that night of darkness and warmth and awakening.

In the morning we had an early breakfast at the Marble Arch Lyons Corner House before going on our separate ways, and I remember finding myself on a semi-deserted platform at the Marble Arch underground with a sudden urge to shout something out loud, nothing as self-regarding as "I've done it!", more like "It's true!"

Ben's flat near Paddington, a tiny room up flights of steep stairs and under a sloping roof, but made romantically Bohemian by some of Carola's canvases, including a full-length portrait of Lisa, provided other memories to cherish before the plunge into the unknown. By that time Lisa had made me promise to keep up the diary and lay off the booze.

The latter request followed my disclosure that, during a night I had spent at the Randolph Hotel in Oxford, I had started awake to see floating in the darkness beside me the head of a negro in profile, the velvety cheekbone aglow from the light of a cigarette stub in his mouth. I closed my eyes and opened them again. He was still there, palpable as the dagger Macbeth saw before him.

My farewell postcard, from Poole, must have puzzled the postman if he read it. "Darling Lisa, At 4.20 a.m. tomorrow I'm off, thinking so much of you, sweet, and your *honey*-coloured hair! Do write soon, darling. I promise no more negroes!! Many kisses, M."

CHAPTER THIRTEEN

"Tuesday, 27 March. Colombo. Kraal Number 45 – my billet for tonight: straw roof, raffia-plaited walls, doors and window open to the moonlight and mosquitoes, my bed rearing its muslin protection like a palanquin. A lizard streaks across the stone floor, outside crickets sound their dry cymbals and the Indian Ocean breaks gently on the white sand.

"Was it only a week ago that Lisa, Carola and I left Kempinski's to share a taxi with a soldier home after years from the wars? A week ago that Lisa and I left the taxi to climb the dark stairs to Ben's flat? Time, space and emotion are far removed."

"A Journey Between Two Wars" was the title the *News Chronicle* gave to a half-page feature describing my four weeks' flight from Poole via Australia to the naval base at Leyte in the Philippines. Tailored to a newspaper's requirements, it suggested little of the excitement that spills over in the diary entries I wrote at stages of the flight, the excitement of travel before television and the package tour had shrunk the globe and made a commonplace of the exotic.

For me the Middle and Far East were places I had tried to imagine from a diversity of sources – the Bible and the *Arabian Nights*, Conrad and Kipling, Flecker's *Hassan* and T.E. Lawrence's *Seven Pillars of Wisdom*, Rider Haggard and G.A. Henty, Omar Khayyam and Marco Polo. Anticipation was in no way dimmed by remembrance of school atlases showing scattered chunks of it coloured in British Empire red, an Empire on which the sun may be setting, but to which a certain glamour still attached.

My fellow correspondent on this flight, and for some months to come, was John Ridley of the *Daily Telegraph*, a fragile-looking man, with a piping voice and trilling laugh, whose sexual proclivities I was a good deal quicker to recognize than in the case of Ronnie Walker.

The diary account of the flight starts at dawn on 22 March, when a launch took our party to the Sunderland flying boat anchored in the placid waters of Poole Harbour in Dorset.

"The engines roared, spray showered the glass of the small windows to which our faces were pressed. Free of the water, we gained height quickly, circled and set course south for France. The rising sun was 'Bon Voyage' to England – a glory of gold across the harbour and the Dorset hills.

"John and I sat facing in soft armchairs in the first compartment, shared with a Royal Engineers Captain and two Civil Service knights, India-bound. Coming down in the special train from Victoria the previous night, we had thought, over dinner and drinks, that the company seemed quite uninspiring, which it was, but proximity at length bred a certain bonhomie. At least the incessant throb of the engines made polite conversation difficult if not impossible. Now and again we would roar across the compartment, 'Is that Italy?' and get back 'Sardinia, I think,' or 'What are those?' 'The Alps.' 'The what?' 'Alps, ALPS!', which, by all that's wonderful, they were.

"Very much was wonderful. Northern France was familiar. From Mitchell and Mosquito, alert to flak or fighters, I had gazed (how long ago!) on those pock-marked fields, those shells that were habitations. I felt again that unaccountable hunger for the heat of battle, of being *there*, that cannot be assuaged, for the battle is only where you are and among the men you see around. But at least, anywhere at the front there is enough to keep brain and fancy active; nothing could be more pathetic and depressing than these old battlefields where the long-ebbed tide of war has left its derelict flotsam of shell-holes, ruins, charred metal, bones.

"France was dull from the air until, flashing in sunlight, the Alps thrust snow peaks at the sky. Sir John glanced and went on reading. Near Marseilles we crossed the coast and the Mediterranean took the dwarfed and racing shadow of our plane, very blue with heat haze on the horizon. Above the hills and vineyards of Sardinia I wrote a letter home and ate another Bovril sandwich. In the early afternoon we crossed the coast of Sicily.

"Heat closed in on us as the spray subsided and we floated on the intense blue water of the Bay of Augusta. At a concrete barracks behind mosquito-netted windows, tea was awaiting us. We had yet to learn the importance of tea in the eyes of the BOAC. Afterwards John and I dumped our bags in a dormitory and went out into the hot sun. Cactus plants thrust their crude prickles above white concrete walls, cicadas chirred. The Naval barrack-blocks ('Collingwood', 'Blake', 'Nelson', 'Rodney' – 'I say, old boy, which House did you say you were in? Collingwood? Ah, C-Collingwood.') ended in a barbed wire fence and a sentry. We signed a book and stepped out into a long, narrow, crowded street, Augusta's main thoroughfare.

"It seemed that every other shop was a barber's. Half the male population must spend its time shaving, the other half being shaved or watching others being shaved. Bananas, lemons, oranges, grapes, bright in the caverns of open-fronted shops, took our breath; women, idle or busy with needles, sit there watching their world go by; a seedy, derelict kind of world, changed quite a lot since Caesar Augustus left the summer heat of Rome to honour its shores with his divine presence. But not so long ago war came to Augusta, salvos from the British fleet screamed across the flat roofs, and the Germans reluctantly withdrew, the same war that now flickers in the hills of Northern Italy.

"The cafés were mostly empty. We chose one where a three-man orchestra played loudly and passionately to a roomful of empty chairs and tables. On the walls above the platform were a number of notices in English: 'Forbidden to get on the drum': 'Not to dance': 'Forbidden to go in the park'. This last mystified us until we found that the Sicilian equivalent to 'park' meant platform.

"At dinner in the Mess Sir John spoke of Peter Lawless, Grand Old Man of the Hotel Portugal at Spa and very good company during the breakthrough, who I was grieved to learn had been killed during one of the Rhine crossings. He had been in the same House at Harrow, and to Sir John meant rugger, cricket and an old school tie. 'Golf? No, I never knew that side of him.'

"At night the long street was slashed with light from shops and cafés, now crowded and loud with music – violin, piano, crashing of cymbals and crescendoes of drums. Sicilian boys trailed us. 'You like nice gypsy girl? Very pretty.' It seemed not. 'Nice boy, maybe?' John must have shown a flicker of interest. They followed us into a café, watched and waited, until two RAF men saw them off and invited us to their barrack dormitory, where we drank beer and talked until midnight. All were bored, nostalgic for home; one, over 50, had been away four years and dreamed of opening a pub in Warwickshire.

"Next morning six hours flying took us to Cairo. Looking down from 6,000 feet we saw the Desert – tawny, featureless, vast, even its recent history of Rommel and Wavell and Monty and Desert Rats showing not a trace. Neither the silence nor the immensity of the Desert register from the air. It is like an abandoned sand-table, all sense of perspective and scale lost, so that I felt I might dangle my arm from the window, rub out the runnels that were roads, tumble together the bricks that were villages.

"The Mediterranean, curving tideless along the barren coast was a painted ocean, emerald, indigo, peacock-blue, the Delta spread green, the Pyramids, just within the belt of fertility, pitifully dwarfed, then lower and lower we circled, finally to plunge back to life and reality on the muddy waters of the Nile. Outside in the vibrant sunlight houseboats are rocking, palms and houses and people throng the river-banks, kites wheel and hover in the blue air. The Land of Egypt. An Egyptian in a fez climbs aboard and proceeds to spray us. The stuff has a strong smell. Perhaps it is Flit! Sir John and Sir Kenneth stiffen.

"From a balcony of the huge Grand Hotel we look down on streets whirling with life, noisy as a parrot house. Trams, taxis, sumptuous private cars clanged and honked and blew silvery horns, gharry drivers cracked their long whips, East and West jostled on the sidewalks – Arabs, Egyptians, Moslems, men of the Middle East forces, men homeward bound from India and Burma, outward bound from England – pale face met tanned.

"We joined the throng, lingering at shops rich, after wartime England, as Ali Baba's cave. You could buy clothes without coupons, books long out of print at home, camera film, perfume, carpets and silks, food and drink. At night we teamed up with the R.E. officer and a Dutch civilian we had dubbed Hackinbush at a cabaret, a sophisticated affair on a huge stage, with two bands, one 'swing', the other 'eastern'. RAF officers lounged at most of the tables, but three rows of chairs bang up against the platform were occupied by Arabs. They sat riveted, spellbound, until the end of each turn when one of them, in a fervour of enthusiasm, leapt to his feet gesticulating wildly and shouting hurrahs. There soon developed a chorus of English voices, 'Sit down there.' 'Down, sir, down!' But the Arab took no notice.

"For two days from Cairo it was nothing but desert and sea. Around their names imagination has built up romance and mystery. But from the air the Red Sea is scarcely distinguishable from the Persian Gulf and there is little to choose between Iraq and Arabia Deserta, nothing but the brown baked sands, ribbed like waves, no vestige of life, for if there are tribes, tents, flocks, they move as unseen specks in that immensity. We came down for 'elevenses' (Bovril!) and to refuel at Lake Habbaniya. The BOAC station on the lakeside appeared to be the only habitation; all else was desert and a silence hardly disturbed by the lake ripples breaking on the shore.

"We drank our Bovril looking through the mosquito-netted windows at the hard brown hillocks. A Bedouin climbed to the skyline, his robe fluttering about him and plunged beyond. But Beyond was nothing – emptiness, immensity. Forty days and forty nights in the wilderness – how would one emerge? With knowledge of the Still Small Voice – or crazed with the horror of Vacancy – of Nothingness? But we only sipped our Bovril and clambered back into our plane. Our books and magazines awaited us there, our cigarettes and pipes, and soon the carton lunch from the ice-box – assorted meats, salad, cheese, bananas, tangerines, coffee.

"Towards sunset we alighted off the island of Bahrain, famous for its pearl fisheries and an important link on the air route to the east. Straw and mud huts, a uniform dingy grey, a few more imposing buildings, with minarets, stained glass, electric light. Is this the glamour of the East? The semi-naked children, turbaned men and heavily robed women move in a world

145

stranger than any we have seen so far. What do they find to do when the sun has set and the long hours expand in the cramped darkness of their huts?

"In the more substantial sector of the town a few shops are open, their meagre contents spread out in the warm glow of oil lamps. Men and boys squat on their haunches around a charcoal fire on the side-walk where biscuits sizzle on trays. In a dimly lit room men are grouped about a table, drinking and drawing on their hookahs. Music wails from a gramophone – wild and strident. Hassan's Yasmin was never heard in our imagination to breathe such a song ('Shower down thy love, O burning bright/ For one night or the other night/ Will come the gardener in white/ And gathered flowers are dead, Yasmin.')

"We come back, by twos and threes, from the night's stroll. 'No, there's nothing much to see, old boy . . . Nothing to drink.' We lie down under the fans in the dormitory as the tide turns on the beach and the surf glitters under the stars.

"For a short while on the way to Karachi we flew over the Iman Peninsula, a welcome change after so much desert and sea. Mountains, brown, sun-baked, corrugated, threaded by valleys and defiles, here and there on the rock plateaus tiny squares of parched green – some man's pitiful crop or pasture – like threadbare rags laid out in the sun. Mountains and craters of the moon could not have looked less hospitable, but this being Earth and those tatters of grey-green men's attempt at civilization, memory dabbled with rock-dwellers, tenders of mountain goats, dervish, brigand and robber chief. A casual curiosity – and our airborne indifference was probably matched by the cursory if highly-coloured speculation of some lonely traveller threading a defile down there, roused by the hum of engines to raise his eyes from the heat-shimmering surfaces of rock. So we, and he, passed from sight and mind.

"At Karachi two civilizations meet, if not to shake hands, at least to proffer, and accept, a salute. Sir John and Sir Kenneth had noticeably stiffened. On the train from Victoria one would have classed them as amiable gentlemen, Eton or Harrow, good clubmen, frequenters of Lord's and Twickenham, subscribers to *The Field* and *Blackwood's*, requiring due deference from

146

waiters and the like but not above a little discreet over-tipping. Alas! the East was claiming them, claiming them not as its own; they came as Empire-builders, as Sahibs should come, with heart and arteries hardened, injected against malaria, yellow fever and brotherly love.

"At Cairo they had begun to sniff the East. Had not a Wog presumed to spray them! At Bahrain it was almost the genuine article – the natives, the huts, the fans, the filth. And now here it was again – India. Sir John was Calcutta-bound, Sir Kenneth to some unpronounceable inland region. With England so close behind, was there as much to pity as to blame? What drab vistas opened before them? Again that deadening round, the sweat and flies, siesta and tepid showers, bridge and the whisky flask.

"In Karachi the Indian customs' officials, the gharry drivers, the shopkeepers and waiters, knew that voice, sharp as an adder, impersonal as the Royal 'we'. It was now a look and a word if the gin and lime was not cold or the voice not steeped in servility; we wondered if in the wilds they might brandish a horse-whip.

"Our billet was formerly the museum. One enters through the jaw-bone of a whale, curved grotesquely above the doorway. Inside there are still a few dreary relics, but the great stone-walled chamber where voices were wont to be hushed is lively with chatter and the padding of bare-footed servants; flimsy partitions divide one wing into dormitories and wash-rooms. In the entrance hall sofas and chairs circle magazine-covered tables, and here we make the acquaintance of *Punch* (the 10th January edition), an acquaintance that is to be renewed at hostels and clubs all the way to the British Pacific Fleet, where finally it will turn up in the wardroom of Britain's largest aircraft carrier.

"We had two days at Karachi, by which time our Sunderland was winging back to England. It is a city which sprawls, very pleasant in parts, but without integral character. The country all round is flat desert with nondescript hills parched in the shimmering distance. Something had to be done here about the heat. Most of us blossomed forth in shirts and shorts. Exceptions were the assistant laboratory foreman, Durham miner and others of the weedy collection of civilian 'key-men', who stuck doggedly, and stickily, to their dark striped suits and waistcoats.

147

"John and I drove in a gharry to the shops and to draw money, grateful for a faint breeze. The hot leather of the seat was painful to touch. The gharry drivers haunt the Museum drive (the whiter the man the greener) and charge exorbitantly. Most wield their long whips unmercifully but to no effect. Occasionally the emaciated horse will kick back, having had enough of it.

"In the garden of a hotel we had a drink with a bronzed R.E. officer, England-bound after three years in India and Burma. It was disturbing to find that his attitude to the Indians hardly differed from that of Sir John and Sir Kenneth, or the Durham miner. He had no time for papers that preached Home Rule or had a good word to say about Gandhi. Let them try living amongst the bastards.

"At his suggestion we spent the afternoon at the Boat Club (whites only) where officers on leave or in transit and a few resident sahibs lay stretched in the sun or showed their prowess on the swimming-pool diving-board. Ashamed to expose torsos not even slightly sunburned, we contented ourselves drinking tea on the terrace, looking on at the antics of the hearty, healthy, happy boys and at the kites wheeling overhead in the white-hot sky.

"On the way back we looked in at the Reuter's office we had noticed, a cool untidy room where an Indian girl and two young men sat about doing nothing. They spoke English well and we invited them to the Museum bar for an evening drink. They came with plans for the evening. First we visited the girl's home, the sitting-room overfurnished, lurid pictures of the Virgin Mary and the Sacred Heart on the walls. There was a piano – they liked American jazz. The father was passionately devoted to bridge; he liked a pipe, too. The brother was an inveterate cinema-goer, preferably Hollywood films.

"We sallied forth again, the girl in a pink dress that made her look quite pretty, and climbed into a gharry. They were going to show us Karachi's show-place, Clifton, a few miles along the coast. It was a fashionable resort, the girl told us, to which wealthier Indians would drive out in the evenings, before petrol restrictions, for a bathe or a promenade. On holidays the common folk flock out by gharry and camel cart. The beach is approached down flights of stone steps and along a pier of shining white concrete, flanked by flower-beds and a bandstand. It was evident our Indians would have liked to see a concrete promenade as well and all the amenities of a British resort.

"Altogether too Anglo, we had decided by the time we got back to Karachi, where they continued to seek approval over drinks on a hotel lawn. Exclusive British clubs were objects of veneration, though they were clever enough to laugh at the club types. They were derogatory about Tamil films and Indian music and wished there were more dance halls offering Swing. In the street opposite, vendors of sandals, straw bags, curios, tobacco, fruit, sat in the warm flicker of oil lamps. In the hotel a loudspeaker blared Bing Crosby and fairy lights came out in the trees.

"The flights from Karachi to Ceylon via Bombay were by Dakotas, the most uncomfortable of planes. They were designed for paratroops and perhaps it was part of the design to make them so uncomfortable that one would welcome the chance of jumping out. Sufferers with us included a WREN, a WAAF and a Free French girl, a Lt General and three R.E. privates, grilled in sweat awaiting take-off, freezing above the clouds, facing each other in two long rows on the bucket seats with our luggage piled between.

"The incessant din and vibration induces a desire for sleep that cannot properly be satisfied; knobs and sharp protrusions lie in wait behind, and the luggage is just too far away to lean forward on. We would doze off in attitudes of strange contortion only to wake with a hand or leg gone so dead that it had to be lifted like an artificial limb. By screwing one's head round like an owl, it was just possible to squint through the porthole at one's back and glimpse a wing, a propeller and a segment of earth or sky. Much of the time we read: apart from magazines, a strange assortment of titles, *Emma*, *My Friends the Apes*, *Westward Ho!*, *You'll Catch Your Death*, *The Story of the Gospels*.

"From Santa Cruz, our billet for the first night, John and I took an electric train the 15 miles to Bombay. Vastly different from Karachi, the wide, jam-packed, raucous streets of Bombay's West End suggested there were far more American than British servicemen passing through or stationed near, thronging the curios shops and restaurants. We dined at Green's, a palatial hotel overlooking the bay. By an open window in the huge ultra-modern restaurant we watched sunset fade from the sky and ships at anchor in the bay become glittering islands of light. The band was large and loud, the dance-floor crowded with Yanks. Before dinner one had come up to me saying, 'I've never met an Englishman before. We came straight here from the States.' I don't know quite what he expected, but he seemed a bit disappointed."

The diary ends, more appropriately, in one of the most sought-after outposts of Empire, and with a glimpse of a hotel as famed as Green's, but very much a British officers' preserve.

"John and I had a post-dinner drink at the Galleface Hotel in Colombo, renowned throughout the East. Fans whirred, the bare-footed waiters paddled the carpets of the lounge, where Naval officers, immaculate in white, lifted glasses to wives or lady friends straight out of *The Tatler*, exquisitely gowned and groomed. Alcohol was not usually served to non-diners, but the waiter, as a special concession, brought us gin with our lemon juice, with a murmured 'The Manager might refuse a Brigadier!' Perhaps it was our warco shoulder-flashes and scruffy ex-Burma look, perhaps the tip."

The diary was not resumed, and from Colombo on my account depends largely on my letters home, particularly to Lisa. Fortunately, thanks to the amount of time I had on my hands during the months at sea, this was a prolific output.

After the 3,000-mile, 18-hour flight from Colombo over the Indian Ocean to Perth, which earned us a diploma enrolling us in the 'Rare and Elevated Order of the Longest Hop', we found Perth a come-down ('like switching suddenly to Harrogate or St Leonards') and the other towns we stopped at in the two weeks it took to fly round the coast to Brisbane, nothing to write home about, Sydney excepted.

Of the stopping places en route from Brisbane to Leyte, Biak provided my first example of a Pacific island: "Very hot, wonderful blue sea, coral beach strewn with the débris of a year-old battle, lots of Yanks, a few fuzzy-wuzzy natives, spearing fish and posing for snaps, very solemnly, good bathing, but after my Colombo scorching I gave this a miss. It was a small island, 20 miles long, and there were still Japs in the hills. No one seemed to worry about them, and apart from an occasional raid to replenish their stores, they seem content to share the island quite amicably. It's evidently the same in other places. Japs have even been known to attend American film shows at night!'

A blow-by-blow account of a cock-fight at a village in the Philippines suggests a wartime blunting of the senses. "It was market day, Sunday, and the Filipinos, an attractive and volatile people, were in their brightest and best. The fights are staged in a wooden building with tiers of benches surrounding an open enclosure. It was packed to the roof but the 'ringmaster' found us front seats. Betting was heated and often large sums would be placed. Meanwhile the protagonists were brought into the pit by their owners. They strut up and down, tripping over the long sheathed blades bound to the right leg, with glazed lacklustre eyes. Now and again, to remind them of their purpose, two are placed beak to beak and immediately their eyes become sharp and keen, they strain forward with neck feathers bristling.

"When the betting is over the ring is cleared, the sheaths removed, revealing murderous razor-sharp blades, and the cocks, beak to beak, released. For a few seconds they side-step like boxers, then with a flurry of feathers clash in midair, or one leaps over the other, driving down with its blade. We saw six fights of which only two were to the death. In the others one of the cocks at some point turned tail and scuttled away. A cock that runs away will not fight again and is hustled ignominiously from the ring.

"The two kills were greeted with a storm of applause. One, its breast ripped from the neck downwards, tottered forward with more of surprise than pain, before falling. The second lay almost decapitated, still feebly pecking the victor perched on its body. The cocks make no sound, even when victorious or mortally wounded."

It was time to rejoin the war, even though a war at sea, where the only deaths we would witness were the self-inflicted deaths of kamikaze pilots. At the Navy headquarters in Sydney we had been given a briefing and had been taken to meet the

Commander-in-Chief of the BPF, Admiral Sir Bruce Fraser, of which bizarre occasion I wrote, "He hummed and heaved and paced up and down by his desk in an abstracted kind of way. Afterwards the PRO said, 'You might think he's rather reticent and aloof, actually he's thinking *all the time*'!"

To most people at home the final phases of the Far Eastern War, let alone the activities of the British Pacific Fleet, were matters of little import, rarely alluded to in space-starved papers preoccupied with the closing stages of the Western War, the return to normality on the home front and the coming general election. Even popular histories written long after the war are unlikely to make any mention of a mid-ocean operation unique in the annals of the Royal Navy.

During the seven-month operation, the British task force, under Vice-Admiral Sir Bernard Rawlings, comprised the battleships *King George V* and *Howe*, the aircraft carriers *Indefatigable*, *Illustrious*, *Indomitable* and *Victorious* (carrying a total of 65 bombers and 151 fighters), five cruisers and eleven destroyers. It was the longest naval operation ever undertaken and the first time a British naval force had been kept refuelled and replenished in mid-ocean by a fleet train, a conveyor belt of tankers and supply ships operating from Leyte. What we were about to witness was the end of an era. Never again would Britannia rule the waves in such strength, even though it was now in the shadow of a mightier American fleet.

It was on St George's Day, 23 April, that I wrote my first long letter to Lisa, telling of how we had finally joined up with the Fleet.

"We reached journey's end in the early morning light of Saturday, when the sloop that had brought us from the Philippines came alongside this gigantic aircraft carrier in a stormy Pacific not more than 200 miles off Formosa. Here at last was the Fleet, a noble sight ploughing the leaping waves. As well as John and I, the sloop brought bags and bags of mail and the Chief of Staff, who gave us another good briefing during the two-day trip.

"*Indefatigable*'s decks were lined with faces – interested more in the mail than us, although our method of transference might have intrigued them. Ropes on pulleys were strung between the two ships, which were sailing at about ten knots. We sat in a kind of canvas chair and sailed through the air with *not* the greatest of ease: those leaping waves beneath.

"The Fleet had completed its first operation, so we're having a lazy time in comparative luxury. My cabin is next to the Admiral's palatial quarters (actually there's no Admiral aboard), roomy, well furnished, but unfortunately without a porthole. Despite fans and air vents it's very hot. I write stripped to the waist and clammy with sweat. We live in a perpetual Turkish bath. To think so recently I was knee-deep in Ardennes snow!

"The wardroom is large and crowded with officers, a friendly lot. Most of the Fleet Air Arm pilots are very young – a 20th birthday yesterday! – gay, sentimental, naive in some respects, ancient in others. Only five weeks from England make us unique. Everyone wants to know what London is like now. Is the black-out still in force? Were the trees beginning to bud? What about rocket bombs? There are no papers here, and no BBC. Mail is the only touch with home. On the sloop John and I were inveigled into speaking on the ship's wireless – he on home news, I on the Ardennes – to the crew of 200. Here there are nearly 2,000 and the Commander threatens us with another talk, a more alarming prospect! So far I haven't written a thing apart from a feature on the journey out I doubt will be used.

"Have no forebodings. You may picture me prone on the quarter-deck in shorts and sandals, watching the ship's glittering wake in a blue ocean – good company, excellent food and plenty of drink (though rationed). Don't frown, I'm eating like a horse and the only negroes I have seen have been flesh-and-blood ones!"

CHAPTER FOURTEEN

Life on the ocean wave for a civilian landlubber, though disguised in uniform, was different in every way from Maastricht, where the fighting was only a jeep-ride away and every day was what you made of it. A warship was an enclosed world within the enclosed world of the Fleet. Apart from two kamikaze attacks and one operational flight over a Japanese-occupied island, I would hardly have known there was an enemy out there.

Later I was to react against this feeling of isolation: "I sometimes wish I was with an army again, plenty to do and write about and the feeling of being in the thick of things and up against reality, trenches rather than horizons," but for the present I contentedly relaxed into *Indefatigable*'s time-honoured daily routine, in an atmosphere somewhere between that of a cruise liner and an exclusive club.

For two months before our arrival the BPF's first engagement, as part of the American Fifth Fleet, had been during 'Operation Iceberg', the invasion of Okinawa, the capture of which would at last bring Japan within range of American heavy bombers. That capture was to take eighty-two days, during which most of the Japanese garrison of 80,000 were wiped out, at a cost of 12,000 American lives. The BPF's unspectacular but crucial role was the neutralizing of Japanese airfields on the group of islands known as the Sakishima Gunto, the only link between the Japanese on Formosa and the hard-pressed Okinawa garrison.

With the virtual elimination of the Jap navy the Allied Fleet would have had an easy enough time of it had it not been for that new weapon of Japanese fanaticism, the kamikaze ('wind of the gods'). From a mass attack of 350 suicide planes on 6 April to the end of the Okinawa campaign, it was estimated that 1,900 kamikaze pilots took off, never to return. Most were shot down by fighters or flak before homing on a target, but 24 ships were sunk and another 202 damaged.

It was only two weeks after we had come aboard that we were on the receiving end of such an attack, and the *News Chronicle*'s treatment of my eye-witness accounts was the clearest of indications as to how much the Pacific war had become the half-forgotten war. Had these been German suicide planes attacking a British Fleet in the Atlantic every front page in Fleet Street would have vied for the most lurid of headlines. The first of my despatches, severely cut, was tucked away on the back page under the drab heading 'Jap suicide planes sent into action'; the other shared equal space on page three with a story headed: 'Hospital ward closed: not enough nurses'.

"4 May. The big guns of the British Pacific Fleet today joined in the pounding of vital Japanese airfields on the Sakishima Gunto. Fleet Air Army bombers striking shortly after dawn had opened the second phase of the Fleet's operations in Pacific waters. Returning to their targets of two weeks ago, they straddled airfield runways at Miyake and Ishigaki with their 500-pounders, while rocket-firing Fireflies attacked coastal targets and flak positions.

"The bombardment was carried out by a force of battleships and cruisers. Some sixteen miles from the target fourteen-inch guns sent the crushing weight of their broadsides to batter runways and perimeters. Two Corsairs spotting for the cruiser force observed excellent results.

"While the bombardment was in progress, the aircraft carrier force, separated from the escorting battleships and cruisers, was subjected to a vicious attack by Japanese kamikazes. The attack lasted over half an hour and was carried out by two waves of 'death and glory' Zekes. From the Admiral's bridge of this carrier the scene was spectacular and confused. The attack had stirred up a hornet's nest and flights of Seafires, Hellcats and Corsairs climbed and circled in search of a kill. Meanwhile the guns of carriers and destroyers thundered and flashed until the sky was smudged with black shell-bursts.

"Only three of the suicide planes succeeded in penetrating the fighter screen and curtain of flak. One rocketed down at great speed and a cloud of smoke and flame burst from one of our carriers as it struck. Black smoke poured for some minutes from the damaged ship, and through it could be seen the angry red flashes of her guns firing at another attacker. This Zeke came down in its death dive on to another carrier, hit the deck without exploding and bounced into the sea.

"Shortly afterwards it was followed by another. Not more than half a mile away I could see it headed in an almost vertical dive for the same carrier. There was a red flash as it was hit and a shower of smoke and spray as it dived into the sea just alongside. The speed at which it was travelling must have taken it well under for I could see no débris, no trace of it on the surface of the sea. Fire was soon extinguished in the damaged carrier, where there were some casualties. Fourteen enemy aircraft are reported shot down.

"9 May. Out of a clear sky this evening kamikazes swooped for the second time in five days on heavy units of the British Pacific Fleet. The first two to penetrate the fighter and flak screen made for the same ship, an aircraft carrier. Both hit the flight deck and both by some lucky chance plunged from there into the sea, blazing wrecks.

"A kamikaze attack is unlike anything one has known in the Western war. At the back of one's mind continually is the thought of the pilots, fanatical, cold-blooded, whose last ambition is that death might also be glory. They wear, we are told, some kind of ceremonial uniform.

"Of the death dive of a third kamikaze I had a breath-taking view from the Admiral's bridge. Its approach was signalled as usual by the gun flashes of battleship, carrier, cruiser, destroyer, and the growing rash of smoke puffs against the clear sky. The Zeke was flying low and we could see it now speeding on level course across the Fleet, ringed round, pursued, by the bursting shells. It seemed to bear a charmed life, cutting unscathed through the murderous hail of flak. Less than a mile away from us we saw it turn aft of another carrier. It was approaching its kill. The air all around was smudged and clamorous with the bursting shells, joined now by the sharper points of pom-poms firing from the carrier's decks.

"The Jap climbed suddenly and dived. It was all a matter of seconds. He came up the centre of the flight deck, accurate as a homing plane, and abruptly all was lost in a confusion of smoke and flame. The whole superstructure of the ship vanished behind billows of jet-black smoke, shot through by flames, as the tanks of the aircraft ranged on the deck exploded.

"It seemed at the time that the ship was doomed, that nothing could survive this inferno. But within half an hour the flames were extinguished and the smoke had drifted and dispersed in the sunlight. Through glasses we could see the armour-plated decks of the carrier swarming with activity. The island was blackened and a hole gaped at its base, but the damage seemed negligible in all that chaos of smoke and flame. When, a few weeks ago, this carrier was hit by a kamikaze, planes were taking off again within seven minutes."

Fortunately unaware of the fate of these two despatches (the second of which was used forty-five years later in John Carey's *Faber Book of Reportage*), I got permission shortly afterwards to take part in an operational flight. Though nothing much happened, and though the last part of my copy of the unused despatch is missing, it is noteworthy as the only occasion I did anything, apart from writing, during my three months with the BPF.

"For the layman there is some excitement in the actual take-off and landing on a carrier. After months of trial and error the Fleet Air Arm has brought this to a fine art, though not so fine as to preclude occasional barrier crashes and other mishaps. Two of the eight Avengers in our formation today were unable to take off, their wings refusing to unfold. They retired to the side of the ship and soon we took our place and roared along the deck to dip slightly over the bows and climb.

"The leader, with undercarriage down, circled until the formation was complete and we set course for our targets, the runways and town of Hirara on Miyake Jima, most easterly of the Sakishima group. We were joined by eight other Avengers from another carrier. Heat haze shrouded the horizons and patchy cloud stained the sea with shadow. It was not an ideal day for observation. Miyake, when it came into view on the starboard bow, was capped all its length by dense white cloud like a snowclad mountain range.

"We rounded the cloud pack and the island, fifteen miles across at the widest point, lay beneath it, flat and arid, dead-looking and deserted. Creeks and bays were empty of shipping, roads of transport. Long since, the Japanese have found cunning ways of concealing their aircraft, in fields or caves or even among the tight huddle of houses. Flak, if encountered at all, is for the most part light and inaccurate. You would not guess that, like other islands, Miyake is crowded with Japanese troops and civilians.

"Approaching land, the formation had split up for their different targets, ours the 1,200 yard-long runway of Nobara airfield . . . "

16 May. Extract from letter to Lisa: "The Norfolk holiday sounds quite delectable. Drenched in sweat in the wardroom, we sometimes indulge nostalgic dreams of misty meadows at dawn, London streets in the rain, wind on the heath (in the Ardennes, of course, nothing would do but the Tropics). Now we are nostalge-ing about Victory Day – how many times we'd decided just what to do at the Armistice and look where we find ourselves, etc. It seems ages since I was in London. I wonder has it changed much. Do lights now blaze, naked and unashamed, from every window? Is some of the weariness gone? We're all terribly eager to hear about Victory Day. Papers out here take two months to arrive. Are you likely soon to be released from the factory? For I see they talk of conscription up to the end of the Jap war – and most people here give that at least 18 months.

"Yes, John Ridley is good company, with a keen sense of humour, though laughing loudest at his own jokes and given to putting on airs. Among other things he claims to be a nephew of Gilbert Murray and to own a farm in Cumberland. One of the nicest officers, who acts unofficially as our PRO, is a young man with a beard who was captured in North Africa, a POW for some time and later consigned to a 'loony bin' (his description). The only strange thing about him now is an incurable tendency to sleep-walking; every night at some stage he wakes up to find himself perched on the cupboard or bookshelf or even swinging like a monkey from a high ledge. Even on the hottest night he dare not sleep on the quarterdeck for fear of waking with his legs dangling over the ship's wake or astride the rails . . .

"For the most part we lead an enervating existence in comparative luxury, one item a gramophone concert on the quarterdeck two days ago with *Eine kleine Nachtmusik* and the Fifth Symphony. How had I forgotten that music could plunge one into this turmoil of delight and longing? The mood was short-lived and forgotten in argument at the bar . . .

"25 May. I have today received (by courtesy of one of H.M. Destroyers) 5 (five) air letters from you. There they were like manna from heaven peeping from my pigeon hole to be devoured avidly in the cool shade on the quarterdeck. Darling, it has been altogether too good of you. I have deserved none of it and you make me feel very inadequate. Arriving all together, your letters gave a quite nostalgic picture of the haunts and occupations that seem now so totally remote. You write very well and wittily and I can't thank you enough.

"For some days now we've been speeding south from our long stamping grounds west of Formosa, Sydney-bound, and no longer suffer the discomforts of perspiring. Most of the men have not seen land, except for glimpses of tropical islands, for more than three months, and it's well over a month since I left terra firma. Sea, sea and more sea, the same routine, the same company, the same walk down the oily steel corridors from cabin to wardroom, so much the same of everything that I feel by now rather like a sleep-walker. People become easily bored, peevish, or in naval vernacular 'chokkah', and find an outlet in nostalgic reminiscence or anticipation, some in bouts of strident drunkenness; the latter, though, is difficult as we are allowed only so much a month.

"Round the equator it's nearly always raining or about to rain but without tempering the heat in the slightest; the rain merely confirms the existing dampness of body and clothes. The islands we pass, whether under equatorial clouds or tropical sun, I find almost depressing in their over-luxuriance, vivid green steaming jungles (foetid is perhaps the operative word). After the cultivated, partitioned and gracious landscapes of England, this *joie de vivre* on Nature's part strikes one as gross and rather alarming.

"There's not much to say about sea. And the Pacific for us has not been the vast and terrifying enormity that a man in a sailing ship or an open boat might describe. The ships of His Majesty's Navy reassuringly punctuate the horizon and all between the waves are cut by long and glittering wakes; it has been a Pacific very much presided over by man. Only rarely has the sense of loneliness and awe overtaken me – at sunset when we recline on the quarterdeck, perhaps after a gramophone recital of Beethoven or Mozart or Schubert, and in moonlight on the flight deck.

"There were sunsets north of the equator such as you have never seen – all the colours of earth ebbing and flowering in the west, clouds in the east sombre purple, pale pink, and the sea shot with colour. This was something celestial and (to clinch the fancy) you might imagine as the sun dipped into the sea and a golden radiance lit the quarterdeck that the bronzed and semi-naked officers were Greek gods and heroes on their couches. A full moon came out of the sea one night as round and red as a December sun, growing smaller and paler as it climbed until the ship was silver on a silver sea. The flight deck was like a seaside promenade after dinner with officers and men parading up and down its length in animated groups."

Letters from home were the life blood of the BPF and absence of them could gnaw at a man until it showed. One chore I was given was to lend a hand in the censoring of ratings' letters. For the most part, written in painstaking copperplate, their grammar, composition and spelling were a credit to pre-war State education, though the content tended to be laboured and cliché-ridden. It was perhaps the knowledge that what they were writing was going to be read by some officer aboard that curbed physical expressions of love, though multiple Xs were common and sometimes there was an odd squiggle likely to be carrying an erotic connotation.

For officers and men alike, the long-awaited arrival of a letter or letters from wife or sweetheart could be an occasion that either warmed or chilled the cockles of the heart, and you would often see the recipient turn first to the last page of a letter to see with what endearments it ended. For me there was a postscript to one of Lisa's batch of five that I was to read again and again:

"Tonight I feel like a character out of *Macbeth*, with a thunderstorm raging, lighting up the sky and deafening the ears (though no cauldron and no witches). It is a time when one is forced to consider the power of the elements and too distracting to write properly. A pity, because I am wide awake and full of thoughts. Sitting now by an open window, with the lights that you ask about blazing unashamedly. Oh darling, I wish, so very much, you were here. I long for you."

The task force, which had sailed more than 25,000 miles during its three months at sea, spent most of June at Sydney, being refitted and replenished, a shore leave disposed of in a brief air letter:

"I've been here three weeks or more and this is the first letter I've written. You may draw conclusions of hectic gaiety, reflex to maritime monotony. Certainly it's been fairly hectic, but the gaiety has often been forced. I would have given it all for an evening with you at the Café Royal!

"I got your long vivid letter about VE day and wished – how much – I had been there with you. I can't repay you for your wonderful correspondence, magazines etc., but as a slight rejoinder I despatched last week a parcel of cosmetics which I hope arrive safely. Parties apart, I went riding in a park last week, my first exercise in months – and how I am still suffering. Last night I spent at a country cottage belonging to a young bearded artist, two other artists and wives there, and very pleasant to eat roast duck before a blazing log fire (it's winter here, though not really cold), climb at midnight to a rocky eminence overlooking a moonlit valley and river, sleep on a verandah with hot-water bottle to a serenade of tree-frogs.

"Most of us are heartily sick of the Sydney round by now and I've met no one who would think once of emigrating from chaotic Britain; the reverse, for most intelligent Australians are heart and soul with the Mother Country and a number I've met can't wait to come to us after the war.

"The greatest excitement for months here has been a visit by Gracie Fields, her shows a sell-out. Can't you just see her? 'Ee bah goom, folks, that were right champion! Now I joost want to settle down in me old rocking-chair, with me clogs off, and get down to mee knitting . . . ' (shrieks of approbation and cries of 'Good on you, Gracie!' We kept well away from the old crone.)"

With preparations now well under way for what everybody imagined must be a second D-Day, the invasion of Japan, the BPF had been attached to the American Third Fleet, with the Japanese mainland the new target. Few were aware how close Japan already was to collapse, largely owing to the devastating American air raids now being launched from Okinawa. Fewer still could have guessed at the new weapon that had emerged from the discovery of nuclear fission.

A post-war grievance of mine, in looking through back-numbers of the *News Chronicle*, was how much space had been given to the prognostications of Major Gribble, the paper's 'Military Critic', space that could have been so much more profitably filled by some of my unused despatches. And at no time were they more a waste of space than now, when he wrote that "nothing has happened to alter my view that fighting may continue in and around Japan for upwards of two years", while ruling out August and September as likely invasion months because they constituted the "peak of the typhoon season".

It was as a prelude to a pending invasion that the BPF sailed at last into the limelight. It must have come as something of a surprise to readers scarcely aware of its existence to find splashed over the front pages of newspapers on 17 July the news that the *King George V* had been pouring broadsides into the Nippon homeland while Fleet Air Arm bombers and fighters swarmed overhead.

For the thirteen correspondents now attached to the BPF the irony was that very little of the news being excitedly splashed around came from us. Owing to the strictly limited time during which transmission of press material was allowed, our despatches were confined to 200 words and there was no guarantee that even these would reach London the same day. The BPF's brief hour of glory was mostly recorded in agency reports from Pacific Fleet headquarters in Guam.

Of all this belated recognition of a British presence in the Pacific I was quite unaware when I wrote the usual unwarlike letter to Lisa, on 25 July, more excited about the new ship I had transferred to some weeks back than about our proximity to the Japanese mainland:

"I've just come from the quarterdeck. Rain, a delicious drizzle, is falling, the sea is grey and foam-flecked, vanishing into a cold mist; a sight wonderfully reminiscent of the Irish Sea and yet, less than forty-five minutes flying distance away civilians are walking about the streets of mythical Japan, with umbrellas probably and listening for the throb of plane engines and crack of ack-ack guns. It's all just too, too incredible. The fact is that since we started this operation it has required a major effort of the imagination to realize we are engaged in war and that within very close range of enemy soil.

"I'm aboard a cruiser this time, the cruiser flagship HMS *Newfoundland*, very different from a carrier. Whereas last time I sweated in the huge wardroom amongst 200 officers, here there are 60. The whole atmosphere is more intimate. I much prefer it, especially as I am living in the Captain's Day Cabin – sitting room, bedroom, bathroom and a very attentive steward. This very spacious desk I write at is decorated with a utility row of books: the Navy List, King's Regulations, a Dictionary and Holy Bible; above it a very large map of the Pacific and Far East.

"Being the only W.C. aboard I have no competition for attention – a kind of ship's giant panda, says the Padre. The officers are a very congenial lot and ten times more enlightened than the young and rather raw Fleet Air Arm boys. My first night in the wardroom a number grouped round the piano while a sub-lt with a very fine baritone sang Schubert, Purcell, Handel arias, Wagner (he turned out to be my PRO). Two very good types are the Doc and Bish (M.O. and Padre to landlubbers). The former is my special bar companion, a

devotee of Evelyn Waugh and never dull. We argued about
the Garden of Eden until one o'clock this morning. The Padre,
deep-voiced, hearty and far from ascetic, never tires of asking
(since my first despatch was passed round the ship) whether I
have 'pounded' the Japs today or merely 'hammered'. I have
promised to 'pulverize' at the earliest opportunity.

"We heard the election results on Tuesday night after returning to the wardroom from seeing a film called *Lost Angel*.
No-one had the slightest doubt but that the Conservatives
would be returned. The news was electrifying and is still Topic
No 1, indeed Tonic No 1, for only a very small number are of
the opinion that 'in the view of this House this is a bad day for
England'. Speculations as to Cabinet, immediate reforms, the
fate of Churchill, etc, are endlessly intriguing. Prize reaction
when we first heard the news was the Commander's. In his
deep pompous voice he boomed, 'Well I only hope they insist
on red rear lights for cyclists.' We all agree that Ellen Wilkinson
should become First Lady of the Admiralty.

"The Japs tried a small-scale attack on Wednesday, but were
chased away by fighters. One plane towards sunset was shot
down almost directly above us at well over 20,000 feet. Its
blossoming into flame and seemingly slow spiral descent was
spectacular enough. Far more so was the sight of the Jap pilot
whose parachute had failed to open, plunging after it through
space, twisting and turning for seconds on end before hitting
the sea in a shower of spray. His body was picked up. And
that was the first Jap I have seen during the entire war.

"I described my negro visitation to the M.O. who was intrigued. It was certainly, he said, nothing to do with D.T.s.
Pink elephants, etc., are a popular fallacy; all such visions can
be explained by material objects – a crack in the wall becomes a
snake, etc. But the Randolph provided nothing in the semblance
of a negro profile. I can only presume it was a ghost – so there!
Here I drink nothing more deadly than Australian stout.

"28 July. A strange disease overtook me a week or so ago,
semi-literary. I rattled off a number of sketches about the family
and childhood. Also about Angela Brazil girls' school (St Chad's
etc.) my sisters used to avidly read about; all entirely cynical but

too full of family allusions to be amusing outside. The office would no doubt be somewhat surprised if they could see me sitting on 'Japan's doorstep' writing about Trudy Pendleton, Imp of the Lower Remove. In our inward-looking circle it would not be regarded as so odd. Last night we discussed books we had read as a boy. I had just re-read *King Solomon's Mines*, trying in vain to recapture the old thrill of horror.

"The family sketches are mostly dialogue, how things were and how they ideally might have been, on occasions like this – Scene: the drawing room of a late Victorian house. Heavy blue curtains shut out the misty November night. A tram rattles in the distance. An owl hoots. On one side of a blazing coal fire sits a tired-looking lady, darning a sock, on the other her husband, hidden behind *The Times*. At tables littered with exercise books, paintboxes, school books, geometrical instruments, three girls and a boy are trying to get on with their homework. A second, younger, boy is eating an apple, noisily."

At 8.16 a.m. on 6 August the atom bomb pulverized Hiroshima, and the war that had seemed to be dragging on indefinitely was all but over. On 9 August, the day the second atom bomb burst over Nagasaki, HMS *Newfoundland* and another cruiser joined a group of American warships in the daylight bombardment of the ironworks at Kamaishi, while kamikazes in some numbers had their last fling against the Third Fleet. But I was no longer aboard the *Newfoundland*, no longer with the BPF.

"21 August: Iwo Jima. As you will doubtless have observed the fleet operations off Japan were a flop as far as we correspondents were concerned. With a 200-word maximum per story and no certainty of that getting through in time it was small wonder London offices became impatient. Some correspondents returned in exasperation to Sydney. Three weeks ago I received a cable from the office: 'Please report to SEAC HQ earliest' – i.e. Ceylon and presumably for an invasion of Singapore. It was with genuine reluctance (as Fitzgerald would say) that I bade farewell to the *Newfoundland* and boarded another cruiser, the *Black Prince*, which was retiring to Sydney.

"After a week's sailing the first news of the surrender reached us, celebrated with a formal dinner and champagne. Next morning we reached Manus on the equator and I disembarked. It seemed pointless now to spend at least a fortnight proceeding to Ceylon for a non-existent war, so I decided to make my way north again to Guam. It took three days to persuade the air transport people that my journey was both necessary and urgent, but, to cut a long and dull story short, I reached Guam two days ago after three days' Dakota-hopping among the Pacific islands.

"Most of the correspondents had already left Guam for the invasion of Japan, still pending, and yesterday I followed on their heels, a four-hour flight to this miserable war-battered island. Now I'm aboard an American ship shortly sailing to catch up the Third Fleet. What I shall see and whether I shall be allowed to go ashore is still in the lap of the gods. I devoutly hope there will be enough big news to convince the office that my decision was a right one, there being no time to ask their approval. It's depressing to think how much work and worry it has required to make a full circle from the fleet and back!

"Later. We are now about two and a half days out from Iwo and last night joined up with a sizeable convoy. It's getting cooler, though flying fish still skim the wavetops and fans whirr inside all the time. Perhaps I shall be able to send you a postcard from Tokyo or a piece of the Imperial Palace or a cherry blossom."

CHAPTER FIFTEEN

'28 August. Eighty miles away the peak of Fujiyama pierced the clouds early this morning. As the sun rose higher vague outlines solidified within the contours of a volcano. This was Japan.

"Seabirds wheeled and dipped about the bows of our ships. If the Japanese believed in the transmigration of the soul they might credit them with the thwarted instincts of Kamikaze pilots. Birds apart, the only activity this blue autumnal day is that of wind on water and the churning of the propellers."

For nine days I had been among Americans again, one of a handful of British correspondents whose presence in 'their war' had caused some surprise among our American opposite numbers. Being an American ship, it was 'dry', and, after the few bottles smuggled aboard had been disposed of, we had to make do with Coca-Cola and coffee. It was partly to pass the time that I combed through copies of *Time* magazine and *Life*, the ship's favoured reading matter, to fabricate a background piece to the invasion. It was used in full on the front page, under the banner headline 'Japan: this is Invasion Bay'.

"Nine days out from Iwo Jima we had grown impatient for this sight. Now that it is before us it seems unbelievably tranquil. Crews line the ships' sides with eyes fixed on the distance, where white cloud unveils another range of mountains. Now, less than half a mile away, the island of Oshima, guarding the entrance to Sagami Bay, towers from the sea. The Japanese garrison on the clifftops have a ringside seat as the ships of the Allied Fleets steam past towards Tokyo.

"Three weeks ago we had imagined these shores as immeasurably hostile – the final and bloodiest goal. Only now, as we head into the shelter of the bay, are the implications of peace fully recognized. This is an American ship, and today is predominantly a day of American triumph. It has been a long journey, not to be measured by month or mile, a journey through the valley of the shadow; thousands have not made it.

"In the past two weeks I have seen some of the places where they fell, backwaters now, where the instruments of war are typewriters and telephones and transport planes. From Manus, on the equator, I flew for three days north, Dakota-hopping among those Pacific islands whose names the years will make legendary: Leyte, Peleliu, Guam, Iwo Jima. The marines who stormed their beaches and sweated through clinging jungles are remembered by the neat lines of crosses, a tiny chapel, by rusty junk that litters the coral or roofs a native hut, by the splintered trunks of palms.

"On Peleliu (with Iwo Jima probably the vilest of all the Pacific battlefields) the slopes of 'Bloody Nose Ridge' are a chaos of blasted trees and broken rock. Nearly 1,200 Marines from one division perished on this island, and 5,000 were wounded. It is now a refuelling stop for transport planes, where passengers can drink coffee in the canteen, shaded from the burning sun.

"From the wreckage of war on Guam, a vast settlement of huts has sprung up for the American Fleet. Ratings tend flowerbeds between trim concrete paths. Officers on the club terrace look down over the rim of a glass at a harbour busy with shipping. At night thousands flock to the great amphitheatre on a hill slope for the latest Hollywood film. Guam is a self-contained city of huts, where slovenliness of dress is a chargeable offence. But its foundations are blood.

"North across the wilderness of water four hours' flying brings us to Iwo Jima – dismal rubbish heap of volcanic rock and scrub. This was the 'beachhead in hell', graveyard of 5,400 Marines, where 16,000 wounded later died. Bulldozers have been at work on its eight square miles of sulphur-steaming rock, their blades even decapitating Mount Suribachi. Now, on their last journeys before Japan, planes land on some of the longest runways in the Pacific.

"Off-shore, the American communication ship *Ancon* awaited us. Two days later we were one of a strangely assorted convoy –

supply ships, submarine tenders, tugs, tankers, with four large hospital ships, one of them British, glittering with light in the darkness. The *Ancon* has come the hard way to Tokyo and her war record exemplifies the long, bitter struggle to final victory. Four years ago she was a passenger freighter plying between New York and Panama, returning with holds stacked with bananas. Since then she has taken part in all the major European landings, acting as flagship to American admirals in Morocco, Sicily, Salerno and off the Normandy beaches. In the Pacific she has participated at Saipan, Okinawa, Manila and Iwo Jima. And now to her falls the role of transmitting to the world the news of Japan's final surrender . . .

"30 August. This is the diary of a war's end. The formal ceremony of surrender has yet to be enacted, but with the landing of the first waves of American and British Marines on the shores of Tokyo Bay this morning defeat has come home to the people of Japan."

The diary starts aboard an assault craft half a mile from the shore.

"The time is 9 a.m. on a serene autumnal morning with the low tree-clad hills round the bay hazed with heat. Far to the north the massive pyramid of Fujiyama towers in mist. For the past hour we have been circling with other landing craft waiting to go in. Thirty-six fully armed Marines are crowded in the body of the boat. But the only shooting being done is by cameramen in a craft marked CINCPAC NEWSREEL which has just flashed past towards the shore.

"Behind us the sea is congested with shipping – warships, transports, more and more assault craft. At the entrance to Yokosuka Harbour lies the fire-scorched hulk of the Jap battle-ship *Nagato*, pounded by American carrier planes during the Fleet's last operation off Japan. A formation of Fortresses carrying General MacArthur's airborne troops passes high overhead, a silver spearpoint aimed at Tokyo. Carrier planes are weaving back and forth over the beaches. Now we have the signal to go in. The wake of the assault craft ahead of us leaps into a foam of spray.

"10 a.m. Half an hour ago the second wave of assault craft

hit the beach. Through a few feet of water we scrambled to a seaplane ramp. On the waterfront cameras were already whirring. An air of fantasy infuses the proceedings as uniformed Jap gendarmes and civil police stare open-mouthed but impassive at Marines marching, Marines splashing ashore, Marines searching the cavernous hangars, Marines merely staring back at the inscrutable enemy. We are ahead of schedule and the official surrender has yet to take place. But the Stars and Stripes has been unfurled on the waterfront and floats above the wreckage of a hangar.

"A Jap interpreter speaking perfect English is surrounded by correspondents. Hajime Onisis, naval Warrant Officer (Retired) is ready with all the answers. How have the people reacted to defeat? 'We have been at war for twelve years. The people are relieved. There will be no disturbances, the people are very quiet. But the food situation is acute. The average civilian diet is sweet potatoes and rice but even the latter is in short supply. The troops have done better, but even with us meat has been very scarce.' How many times has Yokosuka been bombed? He flashes a smile: 'Too many times.'

"Japanese cars and trucks are lined up on the waterfront for our use. The only civilians so far in evidence are neatly dressed professors of English from Jap schools and colleges. They are distinguished by white arm bands and are all teeth and affability as they offer their services as interpreters. One of them studied philosophy at America's Columbia University. With a smile he adds, 'I lost all my money at Coney Island when I was twenty.'

"11 a.m. Ceremoniously the American flag is rung up on the flagpole facing a camouflaged barrack block. The camouflage takes the form of a map of Japan and America, with distances indicated. The Brigade Colonel and a detachment of Marines stand to attention, salute and disperse. Groups of Yanks not posted for special duties are wandering about rather aimlessly, examining the neat stacks of small arms and ammunition displayed and labelled in one of the hangars like exhibits at a bazaar. Other sideshows are the assortment of fighters and bombers in this hangar, where correspondents, perched on boxes and fire extinguishers, pound away at typewriters. The first tank, the first jeep and the first dog, a cocker spaniel, have now come ashore.

"Noon. From the battered bridge of the *Nagato*, 33,000 ton battleship, last hope of the Jap Navy, Tokyo Bay seems to be full of Allied shipping. The *Nagato* was boarded at eight this morning by a prize crew from the American battleship *South Dakota*. The Japs had done a thorough job of stripping the shattered battlewagon. There is little left but junk, including a pile of mattresses which might have been for purposes of harakiri. Only a dozen Jap officers remain aboard. From the depths of the gloomy ship came the discordant sound of Jap gramophone music.

"1 p.m. South of the Naval Air Station we make our second landing at the naval base proper. Signs of occupation are now numerous. The first bulldozers are at work. It was here that the Japanese press were waiting to meet the Marines as they scrambled ashore. One Tokyo correspondent, in his eagerness to get in the first news of the occupation, had brought a basketful of carrier pigeons. In the Naval Base where I write this there is some confusion in a corner where two Jap reporters are alternately interviewing and being interviewed by American correspondents. They tell us that reports of mass suicides in front of the Imperial Palace have been greatly exaggerated; only a dozen or so, including the president of the Patriotic Society, have chosen harakiri. To reach this HQ we drove through tree-lined suburbs and a deserted shopping district. No civilians apart from those on special duties are being allowed in the zone of occupation. Allied troops have been warned that looting or souvenir hunting will be very severely dealt with.

"2 p.m. Everything has gone according to plan and all the American and British troops are in full occupation of their respective districts. Heavy gear is now being unloaded, including bulldozers and water purification plants. Admiral Nimitz and Admiral Halsey will tour the base this afternoon. They are already ashore."

After all those timeless weeks at sea with little to report, it was now a hectic rush to see what there was to see and file copy in time for an edition. There were the first impressions of Tokyo – vast areas of it obliterated by fire bombs and high explosive, where tens of thousands of half-starved families lived in makeshift hovels (an estimated 1,300,000 houses in Tokyo were destroyed, leaving only 370,000 still habitable); atrocity stories by released prisoners; the bizarre pageantry attending the signing of the formal instrument of surrender.

"Sunday, 2 September. The final, formal surrender was signed in Tokyo Bay on board the U.S. battleship *Missouri* early today. Every available inch of space on the decks, superstructure and gun-turrets was occupied by over 300 Allied correspondents. Among them were four Japanese reporters. The whirr of movie cameras and the flicker of flashlights was the constant accompaniment to the proceedings.

"Martial music from the ship's band gave an air of festival as the concourse of famous men arrived. It was a sultry morning, with the sun shining dully through thin cloud. Fujiyama was hidden and the coastline north of Tokosuka, scene of Thursday's landings, was dark with the threat of rain.

"The music and the din of voices died into silence as General MacArthur came through the ranks of white-uniformed side-boys on the quarterdeck at 8.45. In silence he strode across the superstructure deck, through the concourse of admirals and generals, and disappeared through a doorway to the Admiral's cabin.

"A hundred high-ranking officers of the American Army and Navy stood in the shadow of the 16-inch turrets whose guns were pointed at the coast of Japan. On the other side of the green-clothed table the Allied signatories formed up at the head of their staffs. Admiral Bruce Fraser, wearing white shorts, chatted genially with the Russian and Chinese generals.

"Only one nation was now missing from the great assembly – Japan. From my position on a platform above a 20 mm gun turret only a few yards from the table, I watched the launch carrying the Jap representative come alongside. Mamoru Shigemitsu, Jap Foreign Minister, was assisted on to the gangplank. Slowly, painfully, with one wooden leg stiff behind him, he climbed the steps. At the top he paused, removed his silk top hat and came aboard.

"He and his two Government colleagues wore black frock coats and striped trousers. Three Army and three Navy representatives, uniformed and wearing spurred jackboots, but unarmed, and two other representatives, one in a white suit and wearing a battered hat, followed. Led by the limping, bespectacled Foreign Minister, the grim-faced cavalcade slowly mounted the ladder leading to the superstructure deck. There they stood, a tiny forlorn-looking group amidst the legions of their erstwhile enemies. One or two shifted their feet; most stood rigidly to attention.

"At nine o'clock General MacArthur came from the Admiral's cabin and crossed to the table. He spoke slowly and emphatically into the microphone: 'We are gathered here, the representatives of the warring Powers, to conclude an agreement whereby peace may be restored,' he said. 'The issues, involving divergent ideals and ideologies, have been determined on the battlefields of the world and they are not for our discussion or debate.'

"The C-in-C produced a sheaf of pens from his pocket, one for each of the signatories, the last his own. The order of preference for the Allied signatories had been decided in Washington, in this order: America, China, Britain, Russia, Australia, France, New Zealand and the Netherlands. Shigemitsu was the last to sign. 'Let us pray that peace be now restored to the world,' said General MacArthur, 'and that God preserve it always.'

"But the drama had not yet played itself out. The eleven Japs carrying the surrender document filed down the gangplank, the limping Shigemitsu with the face and garb of an undertaker at their head. As they reached the quarterdeck the sky shuddered to the sound of engines. Eleven Super-Forts thundered overhead as the eleven Japs made for the gangway. Other formations followed, and, as the pipes shrilled the departure of the conquered Japanese representatives, the sky was darkened and thunderous with the roar of planes."

My hastily written piece could have done with more colour, particularly the performance of the casually dressed MacArthur (no tie, no decorations, no sword), playing the role less of a macho Supermac than an aloof Deus ex Machina, hastening the proceedings towards the end as though he had a more pressing engagement elsewhere, and the contrast between the emaciated figure of Britain's General Percival, a prisoner of the Japs for three-and-a-half years after being forced into the surrender of his Singapore garrison, and the plump, ludicrously bemedalled general representing Russia, which was claiming full rights as a belligerent even though it had declared war on Japan only a week before hostilities had ceased. It was, nevertheless, the third despatch in a row that had been used verbatim, with more to come, proving, as a telegram from Norman Cliff indicated, that it could be just as much a good thing as a bad thing to disobey office instructions!

"Warmest congratulations etthanks progrand series messages etenterprise that produced them stop your brilliant sagami bay despatch splashed thirtieth diary on thirtyfirst surrender report also tokyo story third stop you have scored deserved success stop oncarry using own discretion until fresh instruction stop regards exall cliff."

I was already oncarrying when this accolade arrived, my sights set higher than ever before. At a briefing to the assembled press corps it had been announced that General MacArthur had placed all southern Japan off limits, partly to concentrate press coverage on the prison camps in the north, partly to prevent visits to Hiroshima and Nagasaki before more was known about possible long-term effects of radiation.

One British correspondent not deterred by this was David Divine of Kemsley Newspapers, a stocky South African who had survived Dunkirk and written a book about it. A rumour that Peter Burchett of the *Daily Express* was already on his way to Hiroshima spurred him to find a volunteer to accompany him. I was the one who agreed.

On the morning of 3 September, the day after the surrender ceremony, David and I walked past the ticket-collector at Tokyo Central Station and boarded the jam-packed train to Hiroshima. Back in Tokyo three days later I filed what should have been my biggest story of the war, and, while awaiting the hoped-for congratulatory telegram, went on to write a long feature about the forty-two hours we had spent in the crowded trains to and from Hiroshima.

The telegram I finally got was not what I had expected: "YOUR TRAIN JOURNEY MESSED UP STOP ON MONDAY ONLY SECTIONS ONE FIVE ETSIX HIROSHIMA STORY RECEIVED STOP HOPELESS MUDDLE SOMEWHERE TRY DISCOVER REASON ETWHEREABOUTS REMAINDER STOP REGARDS CLIFF."

I never did discover why my Hiroshima story was the only one of the many stories I sent from Tokyo that got messed up. The possibility that it had been deliberately sabotaged as having flaunted MacArthur's order was ruled out when I learned that Peter Burchett's 'exclusive' had got through and been splashed in the *Daily Express* on 6 September under the headline "The Atomic Plague. I Write This as a Warning to the World".

But all was by no means lost. To my amazement the description of the train journey I had mentioned in a letter to Lisa as "a feature that may have been too light for NC taste" was given the biggest show I ever got, a two-column spread right down the front page under a positive riot of headings:

"*News Chronicle* war correspondent Michael Moynihan today
tells the first story of a journey
THROUGH UNOCCUPIED JAPAN
deprivation among well-tilled fields
BOWS AND INDIFFERENCE ON THE TOKYO EXPRESS"

My copy of the Hiroshima despatch has since been lost, and what follows is a piece based on it I wrote shortly after the war for the *Inky Way Annual*, followed by the feature.

"The train was quite the most crowded I have ever seen. Passengers oozed from its windows and doors. It steamed and it stank. My companion, David Divine of Kemsley, knew as much of the language as I: not a word. It would be difficult as well as inadvisable to bluff our way to seats. Our presence at Tokyo Central four days after the Marines' landing had already aroused a certain amount of inscrutable attention.

"We sought the guard. And luck threw in our path two Frenchmen, ex-internees Kobe-bound. They had appropriated a compartment designed for train attendants in the days when there were any. Four feet by ten, but comparative breathing-space.

"The Frenchmen provided not only companionship but tins

of tunny fish, smoked oysters and Japanese sauerkraut. Our own provisions for the 20-hour 500-mile journey were one K ration, a large tin of peaches and two sticks of chewing gum – all we had been able to scrounge after our snap-decision the night before.

"In the dark before dawn we alighted at Hiroshima's roofless, nameless station. At the entrance we backed from a group of Japs huddled among their bundles of salvage. Beyond, night hid what we had come to see.

"A group of railway workers drowsed on benches round a brazier fire. No-one spoke as we joined them. Their masked indifference was far more disturbing than the toothy obsequities of the guard. But light filtered at last and we made for the open. The sun shimmered behind blue distant hills. The curtain rose.

"We were walking on tram-lines. Ahead and on either side was – nothing. Nothing but bats flitting above tangled wires, spirals of smoke from pulverized débris. Then light touched the solitary finger of a chimney pointing at the sky . . . the bulk of a crumpled building . . . a cluster of burnt-out trams.

" 'Punctuation marks on a blank sheet . . . ' – the slick phrases began to form. They would be quite inadequate to the scene as it unfolded in the radiance of this autumnal dawn. It was in signs of life that the horror was glimpsed: the cry of a baby from a factory-ruin: the old man under the broken church stairway coaxing flame from a heap of twigs, blind to our intrusion: the ashes laid out on tiles marked with paper-scrawls like bazaar exhibits: the couple emerging from underground, noses and mouths protected by muslin pads from the stench – or the presence – of death: the soldier singing lustily, as though all was right with the world, from a tent encampment.

"For two hours we walked, noting strange and terrible effects of blast and heat. There were more people about than I had anticipated, but for all their concern we might have been ghosts. We made no contact until we found a hospital, relatively habitable. Its floors were littered with wounded, the worst cases protected from flies under netted frames. Officials received us with oriental courtesy and little English. Our phonetic phrase-book ('Can you direct me to the pleasure gardens?') did not answer the purpose.

176

"At length a nurse-interpreter materialized. Over a breakfast of biscuits and condensed milk we attempted to build up some picture of that fateful morning a month ago. Impossible. Doctor and matron answered politely, patiently, precisely. The Bomb might have been an Act of God, regrettable but inevitable, difficult to describe. The doctor had been fortunate, only six fractures. I had to look again through the shattered windows to the place where thousands of the dead who still required it had been cremated to jerk their story into perspective.

"An Army truck was procured to drive us to the Prefecture some miles out. We might have been expected, honoured guests, such bowing and baring of teeth, pidgin English and gesticulations, and a meal of hash and beans. I was almost relieved amid it all to observe bitter hostility in the glance of one police officer who did not move from his desk. Before him lay a small casket. We were later informed, apologetically, that it contained the ashes of his parents, that he was upset.

"In the blaze of evening we stood again on the roofless station, there, at the eleventh hour, to be challenged. A gendarme officer walked briskly up to us, clicked his heels, and, through the medium of a girl who spoke fluent Hollywood English, snapped out a fusillade of questions.

" 'Who were we? By what authority were we here? What was our business? Our names? Our rank? Our destination?'

"At the curt voice of Authority, a crowd of bystanders had encircled us. They craned, silently, no evasion now in their hard hostile stare. But the officer seemed satisfied with our replies – we said we had the authority of General MacArthur – clicked his heels again and strode away. Reluctantly, with glowering backward glances, the crowd dispersed.

"On the return journey we were forced to join the battle of the aisles. In exclusively Japanese company it seemed inadvisable to play an aggressive role at the outset. It was not for five hours, at a halt, that we were able to infiltrate two vacated seats.

"On this journey we had overmuch leisure to observe the Nipponese character in defeat. Although travelling through areas where no non-neutral white man had trod since the beginning of the war, we were treated to a studied indifference. The only exception was a child in arms, who, at first sight of the inscrutable face of the Occident, hid behind her mother and soon diverted her attention to a hideous old baboon in the corner seat.

"Two tough-looking Army men, in whose features one could read the potentialities of the beast, were absorbed for half an hour in playing with the child's toy dog, zipping the fastener in the back, wagging its head, tweaking its nose, with expressions of absorbed delight. It required no little imagination to transform some of the more likely-looking of our train companions into the yellow men of the jungles, the callous torturers and fanatic fighters. It was not beyond reason, however, that the set mask that could relax into childish delight could also harden into brutality.

"Poverty and deprivation were implicit in this compartment of the Tokyo express. The men's uniforms (even civilian attire has the appearance of uniform) were coarse and shabby, the women's baggy trousers, which, by Government order have replaced the kimono, clean but worn. The child was fed on powdered milk and water, the former administered like distemper powder to a dog. Adult chopsticks shovelled in quantities of insipid rice with wolfish appetite. Cheaply aromatic cigarettes were smoked in stages, each puff a luxury ration.

"To turn from these alien faces and the smoky, soot-infested compartment to the countryside through which we passed was to step into the Shangri-La of fiction. In the country of the interior, green and lovely beyond all expectation, and the blue-misted mountains, circling the Inland Sea, the exquisite undertones of Oriental poetry came to shimmering life.

"The barren wastes of the semi-obliterated cities we had seen – Tokyo, Yokohama, Osaka, Nagoya, Kobe – man-made wildernesses of rusted tin, pulverized masonry, charred wood, provided the violent contrast between the old and the new Japan. Every yard of available soil was under cultivation. Apart from the remote mountains and forests and copses of fir, pine, willow, bamboo, the Japanese countryside is like a universal kitchen garden.

"Men and women, bare-footed, with large sunhats and bright attire, worked industriously in the acres of rice and millet and on

178

the terraced tea plantations. Thatched farms, self-contained behind high, clipped hedges, and trim villages with high gables and
fluted tiles showing through the trees, have escaped the 'enlight-
enments' of modern civilization. Shinto and Buddhist shrines
and temples adorn the leafy hillsides. Was it for weariness of
this inheritance that the Japs fought like tigers for possession
of the barren islands of the Pacific, the jungles of Burma?

"Ambition is without reason, but one cannot resist the thought
that feudal Japan of a hundred years ago was a happy state
compared with the ravaged country of today. Westernized
civilization opened Japan to the tourist – and to the conqueror.
Thanks to it one can sit in a Tokyo express running amazingly
to schedule and view the relics of cities and the suffering of a
nation. Out of the ruins and the twisted minds there is still the
chance of a return to sanity. In place of the rifle the Jap soldier
holds a child's toy and the smile that replaces the brute grimace
may be more than an illusion of peaceable disposition."

By comparison with Hiroshima, a conducted tour of what
remained of Nagasaki in the company of fifty other correspondents was something of a non-event, and I was not greatly
surprised that my story of it was not used. What did surprise me was that, once again, a feature I had half written off
as too lightweight was given prominence. Under the heading
"This fury had nothing to do with man" (and with my desig-
nation altered, for this one occasion, from 'War Correspondent'
to 'Far East Correspondent'), it described what it was like
to be caught up in a typhoon.

"This on more than one occasion had held the Third Fleet
at bay where kamikazes had signally failed, had held up the
occupation of Japan two days, had entered into the calculations
of admirals and generals, and, without discriminating between
aggressor and Allies, must have played a prominent role in an
armed invasion.

"This will be a perennial reality when the admirals and generals are names in history and atomic bombs a fading tale
of horror. The Japanese call it the 'Divine Wind' – to us, a
typhoon.

"The one we encountered had travelled north from Okinawa,

raging over the Pacific. Storm clouds heralding its approach forced our plane down an hour out from Nagasaki at Kanoya, on the southern coast of Kyushu. We had hoped to make Tokyo in four hours. It has now taken four days.

"The airfield was another tribute to the accuracy of American bombers – skeleton hangars stacked with the wreckage of Jap planes. The wooden barrack block where we were housed had lost every window to blast. The barn-like dormitory was open to the elements and by midnight we had a definite premonition of what these elements could produce.

"It began with torrential rain driven almost horizontal by whirling wind. Mosquito nets, an unnecessary precaution, became sodden and the rain began its insidious invasion. In the darkness gropings and subdued curses and a wild flashing of torches grew with the rising tempo of the gale. Long before dawn there had been an almost universal exodus of the fifty or so occupants. Light revealed a cheerless spectacle of abandoned camp beds sent skidding by wind-gusts through pools of water, rain streaming through the roof and lashing through the windows.

"Outside the wind was gathering strength, ripping steel girders from the wrecked hangars, sending timbers and sheets of iron scudding across the ground. A substantial sentry box was bowled over, and an American MP emerged in uncertain humour. Our party escaped, clinging to the framework of jeeps, to the divisional officer's quarters, which boasted windows and a stout roof.

"By four o'clock in the afternoon the 'Divine Wind' was blowing at 135 miles an hour; gusts recorded by the weather bureau at the airfield exceeded 150 miles. An Australian prisoner who had spent four years in Japan had experienced nothing comparable.

"From behind the groaning, bending windows of our refuge we witnessed a destructive fury that for once had nothing to do with man. The driven rain was like smoke screening the near distance. Trees and bushes were lashed like seaweed in a running tide around the insecure bulk of houses. A peasant's wooden house seemed any moment about to take off, but miraculously survived the most incredible exertions of the wind. Tiles from our own roof were scattered like playing cards. Across the farther fields massive baulks of timber bounded like sticks, and sheets of metal swirled as effortlessly as paper kites. Lightning flickered, but rumbles of thunder were drowned in the uproar.

"The centre of the typhoon passed, as had been predicted, at four o'clock and gradually the gale subsided to the dimensions of headline weather in England. By sunset it was all over, and in the strange silence the Japs gathered around their torn and sodden homes in disconsolate groups.

"The sun was still hidden behind thick cloud, and in place of its usual setting we were treated to an extraordinary play of light. The countryside was suddenly suffused with a cold, unearthly glow, in which grass and trees and beaten rice fields were luridly, unhealthily green and the clouds shimmered as though at an eclipse.

"Next morning we were shown where many of the troops and civilians had sheltered, the sandstone caves that honeycomb the hills, where hundreds of thousands of rounds of ammunition were stored. A narrow valley where suicide planes had been manufactured had been cunningly camouflaged, with thousands of baby firs and pines in wooden tubs stacked on platforms, looking from the air like an extensive plantation.

"On the airfield Army trucks had been tied as ballast to the transport planes. Despite this more than a dozen, including ours, had sustained some damage. The most spectacular sight was a plane lying on its back, one wing folded as neatly as a chicken's, with a two-ton truck snuggling on its belly, eight feet from the ground.

"The bright, cloudless morning was full of clues as to the path the typhoon had taken. And yet, after Nagasaki's valley of desolation, it was comparatively unspectacular. This is one sphere in which man has outdistanced Nature."

After the uneventful, enervating months of sea, sea and more sea, it was invigorating to feel, however briefly, in the mainstream of history, with plenty to write about, and it was not until three weeks after splashing ashore with the Marines that I got around to writing to Lisa again.

"21 September. A letter from you last night, dated August 8th, full of hot days, evening mists, the brimming Thames. In this dusty spiritless capital a fine breath from the precious isle . . .

"The Daiiti Hotel where I am staying is vast and modern. We have single bed-sitting rooms, mine on the sixth floor looking down on the well. Murals from *A Midsummer Night's Dream* in the reception hall and a Jap quartet at dinner playing *Eine Kleine Nachtmusik* and *De Old Folks at Home* add a typically oriental atmosphere. There is a marvellous bath about four feet deep and almost big enough to float in.

"Many of the original 300 or so W.C.s have left for home or China, but, with replacements, the place still feels crowded. Ridley, re whom you enquire, is still here. We parted company after Sydney and did not meet again until the day of occupation. He is at present arranging routes for China, the *Telegraph* having spoken the word Nanking. I bump not infrequently into correspondents I knew in European battle areas and we nostalge about old faces and places. That was really a far more enjoyable war from our point of view. Manila and Tokyo are sorry alternatives to Paris and Brussels and I prefer a snowstorm in the Ardennes to the sizzling heat of a coral beach. But I would not have missed these last few weeks for anything. My good fortune has been considerable.

"The Jap people are for the most part incredibly servile and one has the feeling, usually unjustified, that they always lie. The countryside, green and cool as a Chinese lyric with mountains always on the horizon like a blue mist, is exquisitely beautiful. Small children, dark-eyed, the girls with straight black hair like a china doll's, the boys close-shaved beyond the rim of a basin, dabble in delicious nakedness in the shallows of a lake or in the dust of village streets. Adult inscrutability is a long way off and they are wholly delightful. But the cities I have seen, mostly devastated, are an ugly jumble of massive modern buildings and wooden shacks. The people look dull and one has the impression that they are playing at civilization and ought to go back to the hills and rice-fields and temples."

A carefully considered judgement on the Japs in defeat was given in a full-length feature, The Face of Tokyo, summed up in a sub-editor's blurb: "Industrialists and intellectuals, talking in their Tokyo clubs and villas, have made an abrupt change from defiance to penitence. They talk glibly of Japan's future while the masses face the blackest winter in their country's history."

Mentioned in the feature was the weirdest occasion I had come across, a grape-gathering picnic organized for Allied correspondents by a wealthy politician, Mr Jiuji Kasia, in his native province and constituency of Yamanashi, for which a special train had been chartered from Tokyo, and on which no expense had been spared.

Not many correspondents had risen to the bait, but I was accompanied by my three preferred companions, a tall Swede from Stockholm, an American called Robert Taylor, who looked and sounded a bit like Groucho Marx, and Arthur La Bern, sardonic correspondent for the London *Evening Standard*, who spent much of his time putting finishing touches to *It Always Rains on Sunday*, the novel that was to make his name. Making fun of the Japs was a game we had taken to playing, and this sounded just the ticket.

The ramparts of an ancient castle, from which there was a view of vineyards and mountains and the small town of Kofu, devastated by American bombs, were the setting for the ceremony of welcome, first by the Governor of the Prefecture who hailed our presence as "adorning the perfection of tinted autumn-misted mountains", then by our host, who delivered himself of an impassioned speech, recalling his visits to Washington, the Lincoln memorial, Grant's tomb, and reiterating his fervent plea to his American friends, "Take me to Gettysburg! Take me to Gettysburg!" He concluded by inviting us to inspect Kofu's bomb damage and then proceed by special buses to the vineyard.

Ostensibly a gesture of appreciation of the hospitality shown by the American and British people during pre-war visits, the real purpose of the outing became clear on the long train journey back to Tokyo. Our fellow grape-gatherers had been an impressive selection of Tokyo industrialists and newsmen who now circulated through the compartments for what our host called 'friendly exchanges' but which were clearly aimed at getting as much out of us as they could that might be of future value.

The lavish buffet lunch, washed down with Kofu wine, had induced a mellow mood conducive to Jap-baiting. The test was to keep a straight face while giving barely believable replies to the questioner, like Bob Taylor's disclosure that his syndicate, the largest in America, was shortly to release the sensational story of a defected Japanese scientist who had been one of the brains behind the atom bomb, and who was now in China.

I recall that at some stage our host looked in at our compartment and, on finding what paper I represented, professed himself an ardent liberal and fervent admirer of the *News Chronicle* and *Manchester Guardian*. He was impressed to learn that I was a grandson of Sir Berkeley Moynihan, King George the Fifth's physician, and had an entrée to Buckingham Palace, but took his leave, with an unsmiling bow, when I asked if he could induce Emperor Hirohito to give me a piece of the Imperial Palace to fulfil a promise I had made to my lady friend.

"Obsequities attend our every move," I wrote in the feature "and one is left wondering how much of what they say is sincere, how much a command performance to be abandoned when the last American troops embark for home."

It was many years later, when accompanying a group of Japanese technicians on a fact-finding tour of British factories, that I was reminded of that grape-gathering picnic, and could recognize it as one of the first tentative steps on the long climb back, and further than that, to an ascendancy they could hardly have thought possible: Superpower.

Jiuji Kasia had had the last laugh.

CHAPTER SIXTEEN

"Guam. 10 October. Arrived here at one a.m. today exTokyo and en route for home! Awaiting me was a wonderful array of letters, including four from you. My hunger for news was considerable after six weeks' silence, due partly to my switching over from one command to another, partly to PRO incompetence. You can imagine how avidly I have satiated that hunger and feel now, mentally, as I imagine liberated POWs must have felt physically after their first square meal!"

The terrace of the officers' club in Guam, overlooking a magnificent sweep of harbour and hills, was the exotic setting for the reading of those letters, an occasion whose significance I did not register at the time. For me, as for countless others making treks for home and civvy street, the time for the writing, and receiving, of letters was over, never, in such an unprecedented outburst of caring, to be repeated. It was back to peacetime and every man for himself.

My batch included birthday letters from my three spinster aunts, older sisters of my mother, whose customary scattering of biblical texts signalled a persisting hope that I might yet see the light and present myself at the throne of the Heavenly grace. Aunt Alice's was of particular interest in its avoidance of any mention of Hiroshima. A long-standing Calvinist belief that the end of the world was nigh, based largely on interpretations of cryptic texts in the Book of Revelations, had been an exciting prospect in childhood (I recall confiding to a school-friend on one occasion that the world was going to end on the following Tuesday), and I would have thought that now, as never before, the atom bomb would have given credence to such a belief. But, though Aunt Alice made no mention of Armageddon, the Second Coming or the Day of Judgement, she did take me up on something I must have written about the post-war world:

"It is bound to be some time before you can sort out the impressions left with you by the tremendous things that have happened in this unprecedented war. But you need not covet the enthusiasm, as you think it to be, which envisages a brave new world rising from the ashes. There is no ground for such optimism. This is not to say that there is no help in God for the nations, but it is truly pathetic, I think, that even those who know better think it necessary to join in such a figment . . . Affectionately, A.C.A. ('God encompasseth us.')"

From home came the momentous news that, after thirty years in Birkenhead, my father was being moved to London, news that I passed on to Lisa in the confident belief that she would before long be making the acquaintance of my family.

"Mother may have pangs uprooting herself from her birth-place and the North, to which she has been so faithful, but I think it an excellent thing. My heart bleeds that I will not be there for the house-cooling (or whatever is the opposite to house-warming) and that my next visit 'home' will be as guest of some sacrilegious new occupant, uprooting, for example, the silver birch whose trunk is completely hollow though miraculously it blossoms every spring.

"For me no view, however lovely, can rival that from an attic bedroom looking across garden walls, a nursery garden – cabbage patches, runner beans, bright flower beds, tunnels of sweet peas, glasshouses – beyond that over grass tennis courts and the Girls' High School playing fields, to the chapel spire and dormitory windows of St Aidan's Theological College. Because from there I saw the year's progression – the glory of summer sunsets behind the spire, ghostly boughs in a February morning fog with the horns bellowing from the Mersey, December's sun red in a net of boughs and a bell tolling for evensong: a rival bell clanged from the Birkenhead School clock-tower, and on Sunday evenings the jangling chimes of St Saviour's Church on the hill, whose bells were melancholy except when they played carols in the darkness of Christmas morning.

"Now places like Oxford, Burford, Marlow, Stratford, are just round the corner of my mind, and I look in quite frequently at the Café Royal and King's Arms, Chelsea. O pubs! (vocative, the cry of a soul in exile: at school I could never see the sense of Mensa – O table!) They cry England with as great an allurement as the White Cliffs and the Cotswold hills. Now and again I chew the cud of my experiences and wonder if I shall write 'The War as I knew it', or 'Round the World with a Portable'. Then I come to the conclusion that it would require six months to think it over in some cottage in the Cotswolds, six months to write it in some cottage in the Highlands of Scotland, and then six months recuperating in some place like Dublin.

"Six weeks of Japan was quite sufficient and towards the end a mood of hilarious ennui had set in – if that is not a contradiction in terms. They were in fact by far the most entertaining weeks in the Pacific. We left just as the frivolity was turning sour. A typhoon coming up from Okinawa almost stranded us at the eleventh hour but we managed to head it off, catching only a breath of its ferocity for about half an hour, blinding quivers of lightning in pitch darkness, startling claps of thunder detonating like flak and belly-raising drops in altitude.

"It will be strange to find my family in London. My elder brother Martin, a stranger of many years, hopes to return from Burma before Christmas. Did I tell you he was awarded the M.C. during the jungle fighting, a bayonet charge, I gather. How long it will take me to come back round the other side of the world is speculative, circa six weeks perhaps, though planes and trains across the States may be congested with demobbed G.I.s.

"A really mammoth thunder-clap has just smashed across the sky – O God of Weather keep IT away! . . . palms flinging against a black sky, the rain coming. I wonder what it is doing in London now, 6.30 a.m. and you asleep. Distance seems less with a Travel Order in my pocket and the war and its aftermath receding. This must be all for now but I shall write from some place like Kansas City or Valhalla, Mich."

The seven weeks it took to get home, via Honolulu, Pearl Harbor, San Francisco, New York, Halifax, Southampton, went for the most part unrecorded, impatience to be back overriding any great curiosity about places passed through or stayed at.

As far as New York Robert Taylor was my companion, our relationship imperceptibly changing from Tokyo camaraderie to separateness as America exposed our very different life-styles. I suppose that I felt as the G.I. must have felt on coming to England for the first time, discovering that I could feel less affinity with the American at home, language apart, than with a European. A warning of one kind of reaction had been given at the outset, when a hulking negro G.I. at Guam airfield paused to glance at my shoulder-flash. 'Hot dog, were you in this war, too?' he growled.

At the *News Chronicle*'s New York office in Rockefeller Plaza, a letter from Lisa awaited with news as unexpected as it was timely. Two months ago she had been released from her experimental aircraft factory and had landed a job as a features writer on Reuter's, whose office near Ludgate Circus was one of the landmarks of Fleet Street. Though her only previous journalistic experience had been as a freelance theatre critic on the *Slough, Windsor and Eton Express*, her inexhaustibly lively letters to me left no doubt as to her capabilities.

My reply, dated 19 November, was the last warco letter I wrote to Lisa, indicative of new ties that would bring us closer than ever together.

"Darling Lisa, It was lovely to hear from you and with such magnificent news. Thoroughly deserved, and I can well imagine with what enthusiasm you are pitching into a job that demands imagination rather than set-squares – or whatever they use to make a Hellcat. Mary Seaton I used to know as Wynne Jones. She worked for the *Mirror* in Liverpool and the *Express* in London and I'm not surprised you find her so congenial a companion. Her husband is, or was (I hope I'm giving no secrets away) Vernon Brown, Naval correspondent of the *News Chronicle*, a man who in his cups is the most acidly abusive person I know.

"I wonder have you come across Alan Dent who I see has become *N.C.* dramatic critic. I met him twice when I first came to London looking for a job, a hard-drinking Scot and rebellious disciple of James Agate. I think him one of the most readable of critics. I imagine by now you are well in the Fleet Street circles and I shall not have to seek you primarily in the Café Royal!

"I've had a hell of a job getting a passage to the U.K. One reason for not writing before has been extreme uncertainty as to whether I might be leaving in a matter of hours, days or weeks. It has turned out to be weeks but at least I have my ticket, on the *Queen Elizabeth* leaving Halifax on the 23rd. I leave New York on Wednesday, with few regrets, although I have had a lively enough time here, especially around Greenwich Village, which has got nothing, by the way, on Chelsea.

"Plays? I fear not, the good ones being booked up and the preponderance too bad by all accounts to waste an evening on. I saw *The Tempest* which I found most disappointing. A concert and a few films on idle afternoons or evenings – for the most part as you've guessed pubs etc. Britain is not popular in New York and it's not at all hard to get into a heated argument which ends, as most of them do, in mutual back-slappings.

"New York . . . My 'clear impressions' will have to wait until I escape the clamour of its streets and chatter of its bars. A modern and sophisticated Babylon, with the emphasis on pleasure via money. London at least has its backwaters of repose, its feet in a non-commercial past. For all its attractions, how I'd hate to live here!

"Now I'm on the way to being mentally and physically dehydrated. A breath of Cotswold air is indicated! But first London, queen of cities all . . .

"Au revoir and anticipatory kisses.

"Have just received a cable from my family suggesting they have temporarily returned for some reason to Birkenhead, so I shall have nowhere to lay my head. Except perhaps the Penthouse of happy memories!"

A conspiracy of delays seemed to dog me as snow and ice slowed the 500-mile train journey from New York to Halifax to a two-day crawl, and stormy seas added a day to the *Queen Elizabeth*'s crossing of the Atlantic. But at least my three seaborne months in the Pacific had so accustomed me to the ocean

189

wave that I found myself among the minority of the thousands of servicemen aboard able to turn up at mealtimes throughout the voyage.

Though sailing in the *Queen Elizabeth* was to be regarded by my family and others as one of the main feathers in my warco's cap, I remember very little of it except the acute discomfort of overcrowded cabins and the absence of anything in the way of luxury. Had I known the facts I would no doubt have made something symbolic out of them.

The largest passenger ship ever built (83,673 tons), the *Queen Elizabeth* was still in the fitting basin when called up, with her sister ship *Queen Mary*, for active service. During their five years as troopships, they sailed over half a million miles, foiling German U-boats with their 30-knot speed and requiring no destroyer escort, and carried a total of 811,324 servicemen. Churchill claimed they had shortened the course of the war by a year.

But by now I had had my whack of history, and, docking in Southampton, was relieved to be identifying for the last time with khaki and blue in the heaving, shuffling, luggage-laden throng pouring down the gangways, each of us with pictures in the mind of what might be awaiting us, each with a planned route and destination. My memory of it all is a blur, except for the phone call to Reuter's and Lisa's welcoming voice on the line, clear and collected as she came quickly to a decision as to what I should do.

The taxi from Waterloo, my luggage in the boot, took me back into a London I might never have left, so familiar was the worka-day scene, double-deckers jostling on Waterloo Bridge, barges on the Thames, harassed-looking pedestrians at the Aldwych crossing points, a bewigged barrister on the steps of the Law Courts, comings and goings through the doors of the Cock Tavern, El Vino's, the Cheshire Cheese.

Near the bottom of Fleet Street the driver swung the taxi round and stopped outside the imposing entrance to Reuter's. The uniformed attendant at the front desk was expecting my message and I heard his voice on the phone as I returned to the taxi and waited. She came quite soon with that warming smile and a wave, and the driver, who had put two and two together, turned with a smile as she climbed in.

We turn right into Fetter Lane, the gaping bomb sites on one side patterned with weeds and wild flowers, the haunt of feral cats, left into Holborn, the clock ticking away as we thread through traffic in the back-to-normal streets of the West End, round Marble Arch, past the bare trees and green lawns of Hyde Park and Kensington Gardens, right into Queensway, over Bishop's Bridge Road and so to Westbourne Park Road and our goal: the dark little garret that Ben and Carola have named The Penthouse, and that soon will be ours.

INDEX

A

Abercrombie, Professor Patrick, 42

Allen, General Terry, 106

Ancon, USS, 168

Arnhem, 87, 91, 95

Atkins, John, 35, 49

Auden, W.H., 111

Augusta, 143

B

Baesweiler, 107

Bahrain, 145, 147

Baron, Stanley, 128

Barry, Gerald, 54, 83, 182

Bartlett, Vernon, 99

Bath, 52, 54

Bayeux, 61

Beavis, David, 111, 112

Bellingham-Smith, Elinor, 32

Bihain, 132

Birkenhead News, 5, 13

Bishop, Stanley, 99, 103

Blackpool, 23, 25

Bombay, 149

Bourheim, 117

Brain, Sir Russell, 50

Bray, Wing Commander Charles, 103

Brown, Vernon, 188

Brussels, 106, 110, 130

Buckley, Christopher, 131

Burchett, Peter, 174, 175

Burford, 27, 186

Bushell, Margaret, 137

C

Caen, 61, 69, 72, 74, 82

Cairo, 144, 145

Campbell, Judy, 22

Carey, John, 157

Carpenter, Iris, 103

Carrol, Pete, 121, 122

Casals, Pablo, 137

Cherbourg, 61, 70, 82

Chichester, 56, 57

Churchill, Winston, 85, 164

Clark, Norman, 99

Cliff, Norman, 69, 138, 174

Clifford, Alexander, 131

Clowes, Richard, 22

Colombo, 141

Cortot, Alfred, 137

Coward, Noel, 22

Creully, 63, 72

D

Daily Despatch, 15, 21

Daily Express, 19, 103, 174, 175

Daily Herald, 18, 103

Daily Mail, 102

Daily Mirror, 102

Daily Telegraph, 57, 103, 141, 182

Day-Lewis, Cecil, 39

de la Mare, Walter, 47, 50

de Winton Wigley, H., 40

Percival, General, 174
Pétain, Marshal, 79
Picture Post, 139
Pilbeam, Nova, 47
Poppel, Herr van, 108
Pound, Admiral Sir Dudley, 30

Q

Queen Elizabeth, 150, 189
Queen Mary, 190
Quesada, General, 123

R

Rambouillet, 76
Rawlings, Vice-Admiral Sir
    Bernard, 152
Remarque, Erich Maria, 7
Ridley, John, 141, 158
Rostal, Max, 47
Rundstedt, Field Marshal von,
    124, 126, 132, 135

S

St Vith, 128
Sakishima Gunto, 154, 155
Samree, 128, 129
Sassoon, Siegfried, 7, 28, 50
Seaton, Mary, 188
Setterich, 108
Shigemitsu, Mamoru, 172
Simpson, General William, 113
Sinclair, Sir Archibald, 72
Sitwell, Edith, 47
Slough, Windsor and Eton Express,
    188
Solon, Larry, 64, 130
South Dakota, USS, 171
Spa, 100, 120, 123, 128
Speight, Clifford, 19
Spencer, Stanley, 33
Stratford-upon-Avon, 25

Sunday Pictorial, 72, 83
Suribachi, Mount, 168
Sydney, 151, 161, 165
Sylvester, John, 36

T

Tambimuttu, 43, 44, 45
Tarrant Rushton, 87
Taylor, Robert, 183, 188
Thibaud, Jacques, 137
Thomas, Dylan, 36, 43, 95
Thorney Island, 57, 60
Time Magazine, 167
Times, The, 102, 165
Tokyo, 169, 172, 174, 182
Tompkins, Alan, 99
Troarn, 65
Turner, Bill, 74, 85
Tweedsmuir, Lady, 46, 96
Tweedsmuir, Lord, 97

V

Victorious, HMS, 152

W

Walker, David, 103, 104, 110,
    116, 120, 123, 130
Walker, Ronnie, 59, 74, 83, 102,
    131, 142
Walsh, Mary, 104
Waugh, Evelyn, 164
Wavell, Lord, 50
Wellard, Jimmy, 110
Wells, H.G., 12
Weyland, General, 122
Wheller, Elizabeth, 97, 150, 158,
    163, 181, 188, 190
Wigham, Eric, 103, 112
Wilkinson, Laurence, 103
Willoughby de Broke, Lord, 84–5
Wirzfeld, 122